MW00775268

At once a playful romp and a ser̲i̲o̲u̲s̲ ̲ of the Berlin stand-up scene, W will treasure.

Richard Hoffman, author, *Love & Fury: A Memoir*

The Friendliest Place in the Universe offers a ground floor perspective on grassroots stand-up comedy, a struggle for personal discovery, and a love letter to Berlin all wrapped in a thoughtful cultural analysis of the potentially world-changing spark of communal joy that comedy and performance can offer. Come for the free pizza and schnapps—stay for the characters, their stories, and the community.

—Matthew R. Meier, PhD
Associate Professor of Communication & Theatre, DePauw University
co-editor, *Standing Up, Speaking Out: Stand-Up Comedy and the Rhetoric of Social Change*

Webb transgresses the conventions of academic writing, exploring what is at the center of anthropological research on popular culture while also revealing what is elusive—its impact on people's lives. Her exciting description of what she experienced raises big issues: transnationalism, politics, and knowledge production.

Cassis Kilian, PhD, University of Mainz
author of *Attention in Performance*: *Acting Lessons in Sensory Anthropology*

Webb turns an anthropologist's eye to the existential search for meaning in this layered look at the microcosm of a multicultural comedy club in the age of Trump. Surprising, insightful, and an excellent read!

Lyralen Kaye, writer/director,
Assigned Female at Birth, a Web Series about Some Bodies

Webb's ability to capture details is masterful, whether she is describing street scenes in Berlin, the social dynamics of a comedy club, or the swirls and eddies of her own thoughts and emotions. This is a journey readers will want to go on.

Alexis Rizzuto, former Senior Editor, Beacon Press

Hillary S. Webb invites us to join her quest for meaning and community in a time of great change and competing challenges. With humor and insight, she shares lessons for all of us grappling with contemporary life, drawing upon philosophy, psychology, anthropology, and personal growth. It's not just a trip; it's a journey that hints at archetypal experience.

Elayne Clift, Editor, *A 21st Century Plague: Poetry from a Pandemic*

The Friendliest Place in the Universe: Love, Laughter, and Stand-Up Comedy in Berlin

An Anthropological Memoir
by
Hillary S. Webb

University
PROFESSORS PRESS

Colorado Springs, CO
www.universityprofessorspress.com

Copyright © 2022

The Friendliest Place in the Universe: Love, Laughter, and Stand-Up Comedy in Berlin
By Hillary S. Webb

All rights reserved. No portion of this book may be reproduced by any process or technique without the express written consent of the publisher.

Published in 2022, University Professors Press

Paperback ISBN: 978-1-955737-14-2
ebook ISBN: 978-1-955737-15-9

    University Professors Press
    Colorado Springs, CO
    www.universityprofessorspress.com

Cover Design by Laura Ross
Cover Art by Neil Numb

*Dedicated to those
who help us laugh our way through the hard stuff
(you Beautiful Tricksters, you),*

to my father, who did his best,

*and, as always,
to Carl.*

Table of Contents

Acknowledgments   i

Chapter 1:   Is This Depression, or Is This the   1
              Election? Mourning a Divided World

Chapter 2:   The Spiral of History: Can We Escape   11
              the Darker Angels of Our Nature?

Chapter 3:   The Friendliest Comedy Club in Europe: 17
              Or How I Stopped Being Such an Elitist
              Snob and Learned to Love Stand-Up

Chapter 4:   Hooked on a Feeling: The High of Joyful   32
              Togetherness

Chapter 5:   Do We Really Know It When We See It?   43
              "True" versus "False" Communitas

Chapter 6:   Even Friendship Requires Foreplay: 60
              The Exuberant Joy of "Parallel Beings"

Chapter 7:   "Maybe I Was the Class Juggler":   67
              Communitas and the Risks of
              Participation

Chapter 8:   An Ideal Pair: Communitas and the   79
              Union of Opposites

Chapter 9:   The Politics of Laughing: Joyful for   88
              Whom?

Chapter 10:   If There's a God, It's a Trickster God: 101
              A Prelude to a Collapse of Meaning

Chapter 11:   The Madness of the Crowd: 103
              Communitas's Dark Doppelganger

Chapter 12:   Fight or Be Funny: The Bitterness of   112
              Togetherness

Chapter 13:   Flipping It Back: Navigating the Gap   121
              between the Real and the Ideal

Chapter 14:   The Hunger for Perfection: Facing the   128
              World As It Is

Chapter 15:   Stones in the Ocean: The Communitas   131
              of Conflict

Epilogue   141
Author's Note   143
About the Author   147

Acknowledgments

This book goes into great detail about what an introvert I am. It's true. A part of me has always struggled to figure out what it means to be a social animal. Still, despite the truth of that, I also really love people, and the abundance of wonderful humans in my life with whom I have made profound connections comes into stark relief as I sit down to make a list of all those who helped make this book a reality.

First and foremost, I'd like to thank Lyralen Kaye—friend, mentor, and writing coach extraordinaire who held my creative hand as I tore through (and tore up) draft after draft of what would eventually become this very personal story. She is exactly what every good mentor–coach needs to be—a mirror-holder, reflecting the strengths and weaknesses of how one is presenting one's truth to the world. Also in this mirror-holding category, I'd like to send an extra special shout-out to my dear friend and comrade for life Lauren van Vuuren, who makes up 95 percent of "Marianne" (the book's one semi-composite character) and whose presence in my life compels me to seriously consider the possibility of an intentional universe. How else could we have met, Dear?

Many other friends and colleagues read and commented on the book, either in part or in its entirety, including, in alphabetical order: Karen Campbell, Francis Charet, Sue Costello, Stephanie Cotsirilos, Elizabeth Derby, Allie Knowlton, Petra E. Lewis, Shanna McNair, Steve Pritzker, Alexis Rizzuto, Evelyn Rysdyk, and Scott Wolven. My deepest thanks go to the folks at University Professors Press for their support of this work, and UPP editor Richard Bargdill for walking me through the publishing process.

But … jeez … let's go back even further than *that*, shall we? This book could never ever have come to be without the support and assistance of Neil Numb and Dharmander Singh, co-promoters of Cosmic Comedy Berlin. Thank you both for your warmth and generosity throughout the entire process of researching and writing this book. You guys have created something very special at Cosmic Comedy—something that changed my life forever and that I believe can serve as at least a *partial* model for what a better world might look like if we all make an effort to be a little nicer to one another for a change. Along with Dharmander and Neil, my deepest appreciation goes out to *all* the Cosmic Comedy comedians, in particular those who took the time to talk with me about their experiences in the Berlin comedy scene and/or who so generously allowed me to use portions of their stand-up sets in the book.

Speaking of building a better world ... I owe a debt of gratitude to humanistic anthropologist Edith Turner, whose book *Communitas: The Anthropology of Collective Joy* provided the intellectual anchor for my research. Sadly, I only got to know Edie briefly before she passed away in 2016, but her dedication to illuminating the joys and pain of the human condition remains an inspiration to me. Thank you, Edie, for shining a light on the power and possibilities of joyful togetherness.

Last, but not least, a booming shout-out goes to my friends and family whose soul-soothing presence, unflagging support, and laughter-filled car rides to the airport made all the difference. This goes doubly for my husband, Carl Austin Hyatt, whose love carried me through the equal phases of confidence and doubt when it came to putting such a deeply personal story on paper and then sending it out into the world. Babe, if there actually are such things as angels, you're most definitely one of them.

Chapter 1

Is This Depression, Or Is This the Election? Mourning a Divided World

I landed in Berlin at the end of October 2017, jet lagged and dizzy from the overnight flight from Boston.

My cabdriver spoke excellent English.

"Is this your first trip to Berlin?" he asked me.

"Yes," I said, not wanting to talk. I hadn't brushed my teeth in 24 hours and the surface of my tongue had a pungent, spicy taste to it.

"You are, what? Canadian?"

"No," I said. "American."

Wanting to be polite, I reciprocated his line of questioning. It turned out he was born in Serbia but had been living in Berlin for the last five years.

"Was it difficult to emigrate to Germany?" I asked.

"Not too bad," he replied. "These days it's possible to move anywhere, except..."

He stopped himself. The part of his face I could see in the rearview mirror appeared slightly embarrassed. He didn't want to insult me.

"Except America?" I pressed, knowing the answer already.

"Yes," he said. "Except there."

I nodded, feeling an obligatory impulse to say something more—to apologize or keep the conversation going with a further query about his experience. The urge waned as quickly as it had arisen, replaced with a swell of unjustified anger at the driver for bringing up things I had come to Berlin to forget. Then again, *I* had been the one pushing him to speak, hadn't I? I leaned back in my seat and allowed my eyelids to fall closed, almost instantly dropping into a hypnagogic state somewhere between sleep and wakefulness.

***

My decision to go to Berlin surprised even me. For most of that year, I had been walking around in a condition of numb dispiritedness, trying to resist an underlying anxiety that seemed to come from everywhere and nowhere all at once. Part of the unease was personal. Somewhere over the last few years I had lost the plot of my life. My professional future remained uncertain. A half-promised teaching job in my field of humanistic anthropology had not worked out due to pervasive hiring freezes, as small liberal arts colleges across the United States struggled to stay open in the face of economic and social forces. Instead, for the past few years I had been working alongside a team of people who were attempting to create a new, highly specialized performing arts college and who needed a cultural anthropologist to design and implement the "ideal arts-based community culture."

Whatever *that* meant. I decided I'd figure it out along the way (afterward being able to claim that I knew it all along). But by the time the project dissolved due to lack of funding, I had less of an idea of what such a culture might look like than when I started. Added to all that, on a personal level, I had just started to contend with the typical mid-life questions of meaning—what might have been if the lefts had been rights, or if nos had been yeses. All that emotional, existential stuff that forced me to come face to face with the humbling reality that I was not exempt from clichéd reactions to aging and mortality. If ever there was an American cultural value—more accurately, an upper-middle-class-white-Anglo-Saxon-Protestant cultural value—it was the desire to be unique, special, and free from the restraints of the "common" human condition.

So, yeah, the underlying ache and overall dismay was partly personal and partly professional. But it wasn't *just* that. The future of the world as a whole seemed equally adrift and finite. Political, economic, and environmental scientists were predicting some sort of apocalypse, though exactly what form it would take was a subject of heated debate. Once, I had thought we could do something to stop the tide from pulling us out to sea. Many years earlier, I had signed up for a weekend workshop at the University of New Hampshire. The workshop was called "Building a Better World." It cost $150 to attend. I was excited about it. I had a vision of like-minded individuals banding together to create a world of which we all could be proud. I forwarded the information about the workshop to all my friends, thinking some of them might join me.

Only one responded.

"BUILD A BETTER WORLD?" he wrote. "I CAN BUILD YOU A BETTER WORLD FOR $35. HOW BORED HAVE YOU BECOME???"

I ignored him. After all, what good did the doubters, the naysayers, and the pessimists do for our future? I was certain that through intellectual effort and indefatigable personal will, those of us with a mind to do so could eventually create that "better world," one dedicated to egalitarianism, open-mindedness, and individual achievement, and in which everyone was given the opportunity to develop the fullest expression of their potential.

A ridiculous idea, I realized with a surge of embarrassment as my body rocked gently in the back of the Berlin cab. Even now, a shadow of shame at my past naiveté followed me. While the belief in some kind of final, Utopian end might have found its footing in religion, even many of us who didn't have God as part of our ideological architecture had become possessed by such a delusion. In reality, when had progress or evolution ever promised us a wholly positive outcome? If author Tom Robbins was right, there was a greater likelihood that, when all was said and done, we humans would be a footnote in the planetary archives, leaving the cockroach and the gonorrhea bacillus to inherit the earth.

So, yeah, maybe I had been naïve, but, for better or worse, even the most belligerently innocent of us were now getting wiser to truths about the world that should have been self-evident long before this, including the possibility that previous dark chapters of history might be coming around again. A year earlier, as 2016 wound down and the U.S. election approached, it was clear something momentous was about to happen, but what that "something" would turn out to be we did not yet know. Would we get the Lady or the Tiger? Would there be the smashing of a heretofore shatterproof glass ceiling with the appointment of the first female U.S. president or the voting in of a bombastic, mean-spirited, xenophobic prick? As the Sicilian said, the latter seemed inconceivable.

Until it wasn't. Until it became the new reality. In the end, we got The Tiger. At which point those of us who had wholeheartedly believed in the possibility of a Better World were left reeling. As a journalist for *The Guardian* described in an article published a year after the election, not long before my first trip to Berlin, "First came the punch to the gut, the thunderbolt of disbelief. Then came the days when you would find yourself going about your business as if nothing untoward had happened, only to recall, each time with a fresh wave of nausea, that it had."

In the same article, a U.S. therapist described an interaction with a client who had come to her complaining of a sudden loss of faith—in humanity, in her country, and in herself.

"Is it depression?" the client asked. "Or the election?"[1]

As for me, I had started to believe that my sarcastic friend who had offered to build me a better world for $35 was right. The premise of the conference had been foolish. I had been foolish. No evolution was possible. The world was, at its core, a hostile place and humanity's heart cold, dark, narcissistic, and ultimately unchangeable.

It was in this disheartened state of mind that one afternoon in August of 2017, nine months after the U.S. presidential election, I stopped by my favorite café in my hometown of Portsmouth, New Hampshire. I went there almost every day. Like so many places around the world, the small, historic New England city in which I lived had gentrified. Quirky, locally owned shops had been replaced by chain stores. Care-worn old buildings had been torn down and shiny new ones erected. As one long-time local remarked of the new construction, "It's like walking through a movie set. Almost as if you could push the buildings over with one hand."

But not only the outer façades had been altered. Something in the town's heart had changed as well. This happened so slowly I wasn't sure precisely what we had lost until a friend pointed it out: "When I first moved here years ago, I thought it was the most magical place on earth," she said. "Everyone was following their own creative path, discovering themselves, experimenting with what they had to offer the community. Back then, you could let loose and explore the boundaries of your personality and be appreciated for it. Not mocked. Appreciated."

At least Caffe Kilim still remained as part of the declining old guard. The smell of freshly brewing coffee and the microtonal zing of the bağlama emanating out of the speakers welcomed me as I walked through the front door. Single men and women occupied several of the tables in the front room, reading books, typing away on their laptops, inhabiting their own reality. Introvert that I was, on most days I sat among them, talking to others occasionally, but mostly absorbed in my own world.

At the back of the shop, the café's owner, a tall Turkish man with glasses and a bushy, grey-brown mustache, bounced up and down on his haunches, scrubbing one of the glass display cases with a white rag. His son was on the phone, placing an order for pastries. The youngest of his daughters stood behind the counter, steaming milk for a customer.

---

[1] Burkeman, O. (2017, November 4). Every day brings some new trauma: Keeping calm in an anxious world. *The Guardian.* https://www.theguardian.com/society/2017/nov/04/every-day-trauma-keeping-calm-anxious-world-therapist-tips

When I had first started going to the café twenty years earlier, the latter two were small children who, on the occasions they came to the café, stared wide-eyed and overwhelmed by the stormy sea of adult activity around them. Now they were adults themselves—tall, beautiful, running the place.

Seeing me approach, the owner stood. His knees made a popping sound as he did so.

"Heeeeeyyyyy," he said. His face brightened. "I have a joke for you. Here it is..." His eyes took on a faraway look. He squinted, as if trying to squeeze out a memory. "What do you call a grizzly with no teeth?"

"No idea," I said.

"Gummy bear!" He spread his arms out wide.

While I tried to make my laugh sound light and carefree, it came out half-hearted, forced. Not too long before I would have truly laughed. Maybe not at the joke itself, but at the zest and sincerity with which he told it. Things just seemed less funny lately.

"Good one," I said.

"Funny, right?" he pressed.

"Yeah," I forced a smile.

"Gummy bear," he repeated, more to himself than to me, as if he was feeling the shape the words made in his mouth. He squatted and resumed cleaning.

At the counter, his daughter greeted me with a smile. I realized it had been a few weeks since I had last seen her.

"Where you been, darlin'?" I asked.

"I just got back from Berlin."

With this, something inside me lifted, as if my internal organs had become unhooked from gravity and were gently floating inside me.

"Berlin," I repeated. The word lingered in the air a moment longer, and then I said, "I've always wanted to go to Berlin."

Well, okay, maybe not *always*, but over the last few years Berlin had crossed my mental radar several times, primarily because of its reputation as being a world center for avant-garde theater, of which I was a huge enthusiast. Berlin, I had heard, was a place dedicated to free expression and new forms of living. I liked that. It was what my hometown had once been in the years before rising rental prices had forced cozy, free-spirited venues to close or, in the case of Caffe Kilim, to relocate to the outskirts of town. It had been a long time since I had taken a vacation, and I suddenly realized I needed to get away. I needed to take a break from the endless American culture wars and the constant panicked bleat of the 24-hour news headlines, not to mention the staccato rhythms of my frustrated thoughts. I needed to reboot and get a fresh perspective. It occurred to me that I could—and should—go somewhere. Why not Berlin?

"Berlin is awesome," the owner's daughter told me, "You should go."

Later, after I told him about this exchange, my infinitely sweet, patient, and loving husband echoed,

"You should go. It'll be good for you. You've been unhappy."

"I know," I said. "But not with you, my love."

He leaned over and kissed me on the forehead.

***

And now here I was.

The cab driver blared his horn and jerked the steering wheel abruptly to the right, causing the seatbelt I was wearing to dig into my side. I opened my eyes and pushed myself upright.

"*Es tut mir Leid*," he apologized. *I'm sorry.* I lifted my hand in a casual, no-worries gesture. By now, we were careening down the main throughway of Saatwinkler Damm with Tegel airport far behind us. An uninspiring stretch of urban industrial zones flashed by, places in which the machinery necessary for the continuation of modern living cranked on. Sooty-looking steeples towered over stubby factory buildings. The near-winter trees, stripped of their foliage, exposed scrapyards full of jagged, rusting metal—unidentifiable items that once had a purpose, but now bore the dull, worn-out vibration of things whose time has passed.

Now that I was fully alert, the driver took it upon himself to orient me to the city, pointing out the various attractions along our route: the Hauptbahnhof, Berlin's central railway station; the Tiergarten, Berlin's largest public park; and the Soviet War Memorial, built to commemorate the Red Army soldiers who fell in the 1945 Battle of Berlin. By the time we passed by the latter, we were deep into the Mitte district where my hotel was located. I noted with fascination that, even in Berlin's most "modern" neighborhood, the city's skyline remained startlingly squat and flat, lacking the broad field of high-rise buildings that decorated most major European cityscapes. A surge of giddiness washed through me at this, born out of a sense of relief and joy that Berlin had not yet transformed itself into a near replica of every other major city in the world. I'd always believed something dies inside us when life becomes too standardized, too homogenized. When the many choices for living are whittled down to a series of identical landscapes.

The plague of gentrification and sameness had taken hold over so much of the world, but, apparently, not yet Berlin.

As if reading my mind, the driver gently punched the brakes, slowing the cab to a crawl. He pointed toward one of the storefronts to the left. Outside of it hung a sign bearing a familiar white-and-forest-green symbol.

"Look," he said, "we have a Starbucks," and from the tone of his voice I couldn't tell if what I had heard was pride or derision.

***

After checking in and getting settled into my room, I stepped out of the stale hotel atmosphere into crisp autumn air. My hotel stood directly across from Gendarmenmarkt Square, widely considered one of Europe's most beautiful architectural landmarks. A cluster of tourists, bundled up in scarves and lightweight jackets and wearing good, sensible walking shoes, milled around the plaza's centerpiece: a statue of Friedrich Schiller, the 18th century German philosopher–poet who told us to keep true to the dreams of our youth and not become a slave to the times in which we live.

Along the rooftops lining the square stood dozens of humanoid statues. They looked down from their positions above—amorphous, cloaked shapes, silhouetted against the bright sky. Wim Wenders's *Wings of Desire* had always been one of my favorite films. Told from the perspective of immortal angels who inhabit the divided cities of East and West Berlin, Wenders's angels are tasked with observing, affirming, and preserving existence. *Human* existence in particular. They wander the city, enchanted by the most insignificant acts of our daily lives. Snuggling in close to us, they listen in on our inner monologues—those thoughts and dreams and impulses that we never dare to speak out loud for fear of being mocked, even banished, from civilized society.

Early on in the film, one of the angels, named Cassiel, pulls out a small notepad. He reads to his associate, Damiel (for apparently, angels work in pairs):

> Today on the Lilienthaler Chaussee, a man walked slowly and looked over his shoulder into space. At Post Office 44, someone who wanted to put an end to it today stuck collectors' stamps on his farewell letters. A different one on each....At the zoo U-Bahn station, the guard, instead of the station's name, suddenly shouted, 'Tierra del Fuego!'

With a dreamy smile affixed to his face, Damiel replies, "Nice."

Cassiel asks. "And what do you have to tell?"

To which Damiel says, "A passerby, in the rain, folded her umbrella and was drenched.... Feeling my presence, a blind woman groped for her watch."[2]

Watching the film for the first time, it had struck me as painfully beautiful that the thoughts and actions that seemed most banal or even shameful to us were, for these immortal beings, what made we humans alive and precious in a way that they—trapped within the boundlessness of eternity and thus unable to fully participate in the finite world—could never be.

I had read somewhere that the idea for *Wings of Desire* had been inspired by the statues adorning the buildings around Gendarmenmarkt Square. Indeed, standing there I couldn't help but be filled with the sense of being watched. Making my way across the cobblestones, I found myself glancing upward repeatedly. Each time I did so, I was flooded with a strange, bittersweet melancholy that I could not understand. At least not at first. But, then, a memory. Or perhaps the dream of a memory, one in which scattered strands of time come together like a braid:

When I was five, my parents discovered a copy of my Great Uncle Willet's memoirs from the early 1900s in a dusty box in the attic. The first line read, "My earliest ambition was to become a missionary-bishop and in due course be eaten by cannibals."[3]

"What's a cannibal?" I wanted to know.

"Someone who eats people," my sister informed me. She was nearly five years older and knew so much more than I did.

"Gross!" I said, horrified, but fascinated.

"Tastes like chicken," my father mumbled.

"It does?" I asked, turning to look at him with wide eyes. My father had eaten people meat?

"He's kidding," my mother said, shooting my father a dirty look. "Right?"

"Right," he said.

Later, still thinking about this, I asked my father, "Where do we go when we die?"

---

[2] Wenders, W. (Director). (1987). *Wings of Desire* [Film]. Road Movies Filmproduktion [Production Company], Argos Films [Production Company], Westdeutscher Rundfunk (WDR) [Production Company], Wim Wenders Stiftung [Production Company].

[3] Cunnington, C. W. (1961). *Looking over my shoulder*. London: Faber and Faber, 11.

"No one knows," he told me.

"Oh," I said, disappointed. "Not Heaven?"

"There's no such thing as Heaven."

"What about God?"

"There is no God."

"Oh," I said, my face hot and tight, a tiny twist in my gut signaling my first experience of existential despair.

My father bent down to look at me. "Are you worried about it?"

I shrugged and toed the ground. "A little."

His eyes fixed steadily on me. The teardrop lights in the chandelier hanging above us created starbursts on his shiny, bald head. His shirt was a 1970's explosion of pink paisley.

"Well," he said, "Do you worry about where you were before you were born?"

His question surprised me. I had never considered it. I shook my head.

"So," my father said, "If you aren't afraid of where you came from, why are you afraid of where you are going?"

With this, my five-year-old body relaxed. I was comforted. An equation started to take shape in my mind. Who needed God or angels to oversee the world when we had *Ideas* that could shift reality through the subtle adjustment of our intellectual and perceptual lenses? I thought my father was very wise.

And, yet, walking through Gendarmenmarkt Square in the fall of 2017—looking up, looking down, then up again—I realized that the bittersweet, melancholic sensation contained a deep longing. Despite my more or less lifelong status as an atheist with leanings toward agnosticism, I apparently still contained a secret yearning for the existence of some kind of higher intelligence, one that might make itself known and answer all my questions about who we were and where we had come from; who might even be able to guide us away from the political–environmental–interpersonal precipice from which the human race more and more seemed destined to fall. Once I had believed human beings could be trusted with the task of building a better world, but now it seemed to me that we lacked the psychological capacities necessary to do so. If there were ever a time for intervention, for a superior being with a greater survival capacity than our own to make itself known and give us a lesson in how to *be with* one another, that time was now.

But, an even more cynical side of me argued, even if such a being did appear, would we be willing to accept its help? With things the way they were, apparently even the possibility of such intervention had ceased to spark our collective imaginations.

Case in point: Toward the end of 2017, an article in *The New York Times* revealed compelling testimonies about the possible existence of UFOs. It was met with resounding indifference. As one journalist mused:

> After a year of witnessing a dangerously inept real estate developer and reality television host sworn into the Presidency, various mass shootings, neo-Nazis marching into the mainstream, and the effects of climate change wreaking havoc on communities around the world, would Americans even care if aliens landed? Judging from the muted reaction to last week's report of a secret government program that may have found legitimate evidence of alien life, probably not. Americans basically responded to [the news] with a collective shoulder shrug and a 'Yeah, so what?'

We had become resigned to the eerie silence, to the sense of being absolutely alone, left to our clueless instincts about what to do next. As I moved northward through Gendarmenmarkt Square on my first day in Berlin, I thought, bitterly: *Bowie's Starman shouldn't be worried his arrival would blow our collective minds. Instead, he should be afraid that when he finally comes to meet us instead of curiosity...or awe or gratitude or relief...what he would see in so many of our faces was the numb listlessness of those who had disconnected from everyone and everything that is not ourselves.*

Chapter 2

The Spiral of History: Can We Escape the Darker Angels of Our Nature?

On November 9, 1989, the day the Berlin Wall fell, I was 17 years old, and a senior at an all-girls boarding school in upstate New York. At some point in my life, I must have learned there was a city called Berlin and that there was a wall running through it, separating families and neighbors. But, unlike those of a generation or two ahead of me, Germany and Germans did not factor into my childhood nightmares (these were reserved for Russia and the Russians, who I feared would nuke the United States and end all days). The next morning, my classmates and I had barely settled into our seats in the history classroom when the teacher, Mr. Betterly, breathlessly informed us that the East German Communist Party had opened the checkpoints separating East Berlin from West. Throughout the night, people on both sides of The Wall had begun to smash it to bits, dismantling it piece by piece with chisels, hammers, even their bare hands.

As far as I recalled, most of my fellow students nodded politely but unenthusiastically at this bit of news. As for me, I was wicked excited, because I had read somewhere that the members of Pink Floyd would only perform songs from the album *The Wall* again if the Berlin Wall came down. As Mr. Betterly yanked the world map from the plastic case running across the top of the whiteboard, I hatched a plan to sneak into the TV room after hours in order to watch the concert on MTV.

All that is to say that European history had never really been my thing. Upon arriving in Berlin, however, it occurred to me I should put in a little time educating myself. I signed up for a bike tour, hoping to get a sense of how Berlin's landscape and its history intersected. On the second morning, I arrived at the meet-up point a few minutes before 11:00. The majority of our group was already there—two Dutch, two English, two Canadians, and five Americans, including me. I was the only single.

"Heya!" said the guide, whose name was Marianne. "Welcome everyone. Go get yourselves a bike and a helmet."

As the rest of the group headed toward a row of bikes lined up against a cement wall, I approached Marianne.

"I haven't been on a bike in a long time," I confessed. "There's a good chance I'm going to be the weakest link."

"No problem," she responded, holding up a bright orange vest. "I need someone to wear this and always be last in line so I don't leave anyone behind." She looked over at the couple from Amsterdam. "I can't give it to the Dutch, they always fly ahead of everyone."

I didn't love the idea of having a job to do—I was supposed to be on vacation, after all—but on the other hand, I reasoned, by donning orange neon, I had a slightly smaller chance of getting flattened by a cab.

"Gotcha," I said, reaching out for The Vest.

***

Historian Roger Moorehouse wrote of Berlin:

> If one were looking for single location—focal point—for the bloody trials and tribulations of the 20th century, then one would have to look no further. From the bullet-scarred buildings to the lingering shadows of totalitarian regimes, Berlin experienced world events not as something remote or imperceptible, but rather as immediate, tangible and very real.[1]

The next few hours revealed the truth of Moorehouse's statement. The city of Berlin was a living museum, a sprawling cenotaph pointing to a time that had long since passed, but which nevertheless felt very close by, as if time were a loose and looping thing—not linear and brittle, but malleable and constantly twisting backward upon itself. On the tour, Marianne drew our attention to the bullet holes pockmarking buildings across Berlin. She oriented us to where the Berlin Wall had once separated East from West. She guided us to the church at which Rev. Dr. Martin Luther King, Jr. had urged an overflowing crowd to remember that reconciliation comes when people tear down the dividing wall of hostility separating us.

Another of King's more famous sayings was that "The arc of the moral universe is long, but it bends toward justice." Once, I had believed

---

[1] Moorehouse, R. (2012). *Berlin at war*. New York: Basic Books, xiii.

this to be. Counted on the idea that we could bend history to our will. But with world events as they were, I was no longer so sure. Instead, I was beginning to think that the moral arc of the universe moved like a Möbius strip, an infinite loop in which the present flipped over onto its belly to become the past over and over again. An insane loop of negative progression.

The Berlin Wall had come down. And, yet, back home, there was talk of another wall being built. I mentioned this to the group at one of our stops.

"At least history shows us that walls don't last forever," someone responded, and this made me angry, for Berlin was proof that even when physical walls are removed, they leave behind echoes that carry forth into the future. Generations are born in the shadow of a country's past misdeeds, carrying that inheritance with them, hoping someday the debt will be repaid, the balance restored, and the sins of their ancestors fully forgiven.

When the subject of the recent U.S. presidential election inevitably came up, Marianne informed us that on the morning after the votes had been tallied, her wife had woken her to tell her the results.

"I refused to believe her," Marianne said. "We got into a huge fight."

When traveling overseas, I had always been somewhat surprised at the degree to which non-Americans were aware of and invested in American politics, even during less dramatic times than this. Later I would read a *Rolling Stone* interview with U2's Bono that offered a perspective on this phenomenon:

> America is an idea...and it's a great idea. And the world feels a stake in that idea. We want you, it, to succeed, which is why we become fucking obnoxious and shoot our mouths off about it. The world needs America to succeed, now more than ever.[2]

Pretty extraordinary, really: Nearly two and a half centuries after the great American experiment began, and the world was still holding its breath to see what choices we would make about the kind of world in which we wished to live.

***

---

[2] Wenner, J.S. (2017, December 27). Bono: The Rolling Stone interview. *Rolling Stone.* https://www.rollingstone.com/music/music-features/bono-the-rolling-stone-interview-3-203774/

As it turned out, I wasn't the slowest rider on the bike tour after all. Actually, I rode strong and fast (not like the Dutch though...they were tireless, those beautiful, blonde maniacs, zipping through traffic while the rest of us looked around nervously crossing the busy *Straßen*). Although I could have easily outpaced most of the people on the tour, since The Vest and I were supposed to be holding up the rear, I had to rein in my desire to race ahead.

Two members of our group were not only slow but had the tendency to dawdle and linger, even after Marianne and the rest of the group had jumped on their bikes and pedaled off toward the next site.

"You can go ahead," one of them told me, pulling out his camera.

"No, I can't," I replied, feeling like a fucking hall monitor. "I'm wearing The Vest. I'm supposed to be the last in line."

He shrugged and continued taking his photo.

When the others were out of earshot, I approached Marianne again, feeling slightly embarrassed. I asked her if I could pass "Vest Duty" along to someone else.

"How come?" she asked, her wheat-colored eyebrows rising. I explained my frustration with the dawdlers. When Marianne frowned at this, I shrank back slightly, assuming she was annoyed with me for reneging on my commitment. She looked over at the rest of our group scattered along the length of one of the remaining sections of The Wall and shook her head, exasperated.

"I don't blame you. That guy over there...yeah, the one in the blue turtleneck...keeps asking me how many stops we have left." Marianne clenched her fists and spoke through gritted teeth. "I'm about to punch him. Seriously! *Punch him!*"

I laughed out loud. And decided I really, really liked Marianne.

When she looked back at me, her face had softened.

"Of course, you can switch off."

I offered to hold onto the position for another few stops.

"Uh-uh," she said. "Let's get you out of that thing right now."

When the rest of the group returned, she asked for a volunteer to wear The Vest. One of the Americans in the group thrust his hand up in the air immediately, looking pleased at being given this responsibility. From that point on, I rode up front—way behind Marianne and the Dutch, but right up close to the Brits.

Around lunchtime, we stopped outside the Memorial to the Murdered Jews of Europe. Most of the rest of the group skedaddled across the street, disappearing into the memorial's labyrinthine field of dark-gray monoliths. I spotted Marianne sitting alone at a nearby café table, eating a sandwich out of a plastic container.

Maybe she's happy to have a few minutes to herself, I thought, projecting my own preference for long, uninterrupted moments of silence upon her. I deliberated for another moment, then approached. Marianne looked up, squinting at me through the sunlight. I asked if I could join her.

"As long as you don't mind if I eat while we talk," she said.

I didn't. We chatted as she chewed on a dry-looking peanut butter sandwich. It turned out Marianne was only a few years younger than me, and originally from South Africa. In her pre-Berlin life, she worked as a history professor at a university in Cape Town. We traded stories about meeting our spouses, compared notes about our past work in academia, discovering both of us had, for various reasons, moved away from our original goals of teaching careers. She spoke about visiting Berlin for the first time while on a research fellowship years earlier, and how the city had immediately worked its charms on her, to the point that now she couldn't imagine living anywhere else.

In a moment of surprising emotional candor for two people who had just met, but which somehow didn't seem strange or out of place at all, Marianne confided: "It's difficult to describe why this ugly, strange city has utterly taken hold of me. I'm still figuring it out. I have never felt so free as I do here."

"Free?" I asked.

"There's very little pressure," Marianne responded. "No expected endgame. In some ways that feeling comes from the place itself—the buildings and roads and all the history intertwined. I mean, it *is* that, but it's more than that. It's just..." After a long, slow exhale, she said. "It's so many things grabbing my heart."

She looked at me with suspicious eyes, as if expecting judgment.

"That sounds terribly vague, doesn't it?" she said, cautiously, and I felt a surge of protectiveness toward her, along with a desire to assure her how much I truly did understand.

"Not at all," I told her, thinking about how I had once felt the same way about my hometown. "There's a quote by Anaïs Nin that I've always loved. It goes, 'One always, sooner or later, comes upon a city which is an image of one's inner city...an image of the inner self.'[3]

A delivery truck rumbled by.

---

[3] Nin, A. (1969). *The diary of Anaïs Nin, 1934–1939.* New York: Mariner Books, 74.

"I've experienced that connection to places before," I continued when it had passed. "For me it's the feeling that that place was made specifically for you, because it perfectly reflects an inner essence of who you most naturally are."

"Yes, exactly," Marianne answered in a wistful tone.

"It's a powerful, strange feeling," I said. "Someone—I can't remember who—used the term 'the poetics of space.'"

"That was Bachelard," she replied immediately, and I nodded eagerly.

"Maybe that's why it's so hard to put a connection with a place into words," I said. "Because the only way to describe it is through poetry."

Marianne stared at me, and though her gaze was kind, it lasted long enough that I began to squirm. "I like that," she said, finally. She nodded decisively, almost to herself. "Yes, I like that quite a lot."

***

At the end of the tour, Marianne and I exchanged contact information. I assumed that would be the end of it. Experience had taught me that after such brief encounters people almost never follow through with promises to keep in touch. And so I was happily surprised when, just a few hours after the tour ended, I received an email from her.

> *Dear Hillary,*
> *It was so lovely to meet and talk today. I wish I could spend more time with you while you're here in Berlin, but I am completely flat out with tours this week. But it would be a pleasure to carry on the dialogue somehow. Here is my email address. Be safe and please do give a shout if you need anything or run into any trouble!*
> *With warmest wishes,*
> *Marianne*

I was touched that she had reached out, and sorry that this would more than likely be the end of it. But I was grateful for this encounter, no matter how fleeting. Such moments of confluence and connection always relieved the subtle anxiety perpetually existing within me. Compelling me to reconsider the possibility of an intelligently designed universe, one that had imbued human beings with an irresistible magnetism that pulled us together, attempting to recombine what the Big Bang had blown apart.

Chapter 3

The Friendliest Comedy Club in Europe: Or How I Stopped Being Such an Elitist Snob and Learned to Love Stand-Up

Over the next few days in Berlin, I spent my daylight hours walking around the city—going to museums, tasting new foods (*currywurst!*), and taking photo after photo of the snaking, multi-colored graffiti that swam across the city's cracked structures. After dark, I attended various avant-garde theater shows—a different one every night. I spent an evening at Komische Oper, Berlin's "Strange Opera," watching with admiration as live performers interacted, completely synchronized, with an animated screen behind them. I saw a play at Maxim Gorki, the neo-classical theater named for the Soviet socialist–realist author known for his sympathetic descriptions of society's outcasts. In a building nestled inside a courtyard just north of Hackescher Markt, I marveled at the twisting of human muscle and bone as a local circus troupe bent and tumbled in rhythmic patterns across the stage.

Berlin's theater scene was all its reputation made it out to be: wild and inventive, untethered to tradition, full of color and sound. And, yet, as wonderful and admirable as it all was, I found myself feeling let down, still uninspired and anxious. I had not achieved the liftoff I desired. A voice inside me asked: *What is it you expect from a work of art, Hillary? Revelation? Transcendence? A moment when an act of creativity reveals some sort of Ultimate Idea and the soul of the world is saved? When* your *soul is saved?*

Yes, another voice within me responded, almost defiantly. *Exactly that. Why not that?*

I had bought tickets to shows for almost every night I was in Berlin, but had left one evening free. A wild card. That Thursday evening, I sat in my hotel room, fighting against laziness and inertia, trying to resist the urge to lie in bed watching reruns of *Family Guy*, which seemed to be the only thing playing on the single English-speaking channel.

Determined not to succumb to hotel coma, I grabbed my smartphone and searched: "Things to do in Berlin tonight."

One of the first items listed was an advertisement for a stand-up comedy venue.

"Free pizza and shots!" the ad boasted.

I grimaced. On the few occasions I had been to comedy clubs in the United States, I found them to be overly harsh, with everyone, both audience and comedians, becoming drunk and venomous toward one another. In a world already inundated with trolls seeking validation through snark and verbal unkindness, why would I subject myself to more of the same?

Also, I confess I had always been a bit of a snob about stand-up. I considered it a lesser form of theater. But, in the end, that was what got me out the hotel door with the club's address plugged into my GPS. It occurred to me an evening of stand-up might be exactly what I needed: a cultural palate cleanser that would help me get greater enjoyment...and, dare I say it, more revelation...out of the "serious" performances I'd come to Berlin to experience.

After all, I thought, the lower one goes on the diving board, the higher upward one can fly. Perhaps there was still a chance I could be blown beyond the heliosphere of my own tired (and tiring) thoughts. Enough, at least, so that I could go home partially cleansed of cynicism, able to reboot my attitude toward my own life and our current place in history. I grabbed my coat and hat and headed out the door before I could change my mind.

Outside in the cold, dark night, my GPS led me northward across a bridge straddling the Spree. On each side of the span stood more humanoid statues—winged beings carved out of white stone. The streetlamps lining the walkway hit the statues in such a way that they created near-perfect shadows on the pavement, giving the impression each one was actually two—white marble floating above while a dark doppelgänger crawled across the sidewalk below.

One angel that had fallen; one that had not.

***

Twenty minutes later, with my GPS assuring me I was only a few hundred feet from my destination, a distended scream sliced open the dark, still night. Deep, male, and possessed of an unselfconscious atonality, it was a scream that could only have come from a mind not right with the world. It was a gut-freezing sound, and for a brief moment I considered turning around, hailing a cab, going back to the hotel.

No way, baby doll, an impatient, irritated voice inside me huffed. *No fucking way.*

I had learned to obey this voice, so I kept moving forward, my arms swinging in an imitation of relaxation and confidence. Back in college, at New York University, we called this "walking with purpose." We had been told it signaled to whatever monsters lay in wait ahead of us that we were not to be trifled with. A silly idea, maybe, but old postures, old delusions of what kept one safe and whole were psychologically comforting, even if not particularly realistic.

Just beyond the intersection at Hirtenstraße, Rosa-Luxemburg-Straße curved to the left. On the other side of the curve, the world transformed from wind-whispering darkness to a condition of absolute human aliveness. Ahead of me, the pale façade of the Volksbühne Theater, the "People's Theater," gleamed ghostly against the carbon-colored sky. Directly across from it, on the other side of the street, a dozen or so young men and women stood on the sidewalk outside a brightly lit bar. These dewy young things chatted enthusiastically, sipped their drinks, and sucked sensually on blue-tipped e-cigarettes. Twenty feet beyond them stood a man with a drooping, dirt-smeared wreck of a face. He swayed back and forth under the blue light of the Rosa-Luxemburg U-Bahn station entryway. As I watched, he pulled in a long, ragged inhale, threw his head back, and unleashed another discordant stream of wounded accusations at the sky. The young women and men at the bar glanced over at him, briefly discussing his plight before resuming their earlier conversations.

I scanned the block for a sign pointing to the comedy club but saw nothing. I had just made up my mind to venture inside the bar to inquire when a man with a greying ginger goatee emerged out of a hidden doorway. He lit a cigarette—this time the old-fashioned kind requiring actual flame rather than a cold USB port—and leaned casually backward against the wall. The look on his face was mellow, contemplative, Buddha-esque. The black T-shirt he wore left his pale arms exposed, yet he didn't seem bothered by the chill of the evening air.

As I moved closer, the logo on his T-shirt came into focus. "Cosmic Comedy," it read. Seeing this, I relaxed a little and strode up to him. Pointed at his shirt.

"I guess I found what I'm looking for," I said, not bothering to hide the relief in my voice. After all, who cared what impression I made? I was a stranger. In a few days I would be gone, never to be back in Berlin again. It was a blissful feeling for an introvert like me: being a nobody in a nowhere-in-particular place, wrapped in a psychological cloak of anonymity. There was freedom in it.

"Yar, you did," the smoking guy agreed in a rough Scottish brogue, then grabbed the handle of the door and held it open. A cool whoosh of air pushed at my back as the door to the street closed behind me.

On the other side of the threshold, I found myself at the top of a long, dark descending staircase. Easy, bubbling laughter floated up from the unseen space below, followed by the bright, happy ping of glasses touching together. At the sound of it, some anxious part of me rose to the surface, and with it the sudden certainty that I had made the wrong choice, that there was a better, more exciting, more appropriate place for me to spend the evening. I moved to pull out my cell phone with the intent to search for other options, then stopped, disgusted with myself. There would always be a "somewhere else." One could follow such compulsive thoughts into oblivion, becoming a perpetual motion machine, never resting or finding a spot to simply *be*.

Fuck it, I decided, and descended.

At the bottom of the stairs, I turned a sharp corner and nearly collided with a small group of men and women clustered around a high-top table. The three of them lifted shots of yellow-tinged liquid into the air, toasting one another's health before tossing them down their throats. Sitting at the table cheering them on was a man of indeterminate age with medium-dark skin and shiny, black hair pulled into a ponytail that ended just below the base of his neck. The man extended one of his long, slim arms and pointed toward a tray sitting nearby.

"Put those empties there, buddies!" he said to the group in a contagiously cheerful Brummie English accent. "Yeah, right there." This was followed by a query: "Do you all live in Berlin?"

All but one nodded.

"Then take one of these," he said, handing each of them a small card. "These are 'We Love You' cards. Every time you come here, get a stamp, and when you fill your card you get free stuff!" Now directing his attention to the guy who had not nodded, he asked, "You're not from Berlin? Where are you from, mate?"

The man mumbled something, to which the guy at the table responded, "Uh-huh. Well, take the card anyway, because we have had people who have only been in Berlin for a week come to four shows. Fuck yeah!"

The easy familiarity with which Guy-At-The-Table addressed the group tickled me. The effervescent melody of his voice led to associations of good times and lightheartedness. I barked a laugh, surprising myself.

"Let me quickly orient you," Guy-At-The-Table was saying. "Tonight is an open mic, a mix of new and experienced comedians. There's no smoking in the club. The pizza's coming. It should get here about half eight. It's really good. The pizza alone is worth eight Euros." He continued, "We've got a bar! We've got toilets! If you have any questions or any queries, talk to me. Or Neil, the co-promoter. Or anyone else wearing one of these T-shirts. Otherwise, get in there and have fun!"

"How many shots do we get?" the guy who was not from Berlin asked.

"One to begin with," Guy-At-The-Table told him. "Especially since you're Russian. I don't want no trouble. Haha! Okay, have a good time, buddies!"

The trio moved away, disappearing into the main space. Guy-At-The-Table made a few quick marks on a sheet lying in front of him, then looked up. Seeing me, he flashed a warm smile, his creamy white teeth picking up a golden glow from the floor lamp next to him. I offered him a shy grin in return.

"Hello there!" he said, cheerfully. "Welcome to Cosmic Comedy!" Pointing to the tray of shot glasses, he said, "Help yourself to some Schnapps! It's apple. It's reeeaaallly good."

"No, thank you," I said. Over the last few years, whenever I drank alcohol, my face turned red and made me feel as though I was burning up from the inside out. The hormonal shifts of midlife, I assumed. It was like going through a second adolescence, in which one's body became a brand new entity with only minimal instructions for its care and feeding. I tensed slightly, awaiting Guy-At-The-Table's inevitable push for me to take one and was startled when instead of doing so, he reached over and grabbed a wax-paper-covered lollipop out of a bowl on the table in front of him.

"Have one of these then!" he said, thrusting it toward me. Scanning the table in front of him, Guy-At-The-Table pinched a sticker off the top of a small pile. On the sticker was the Cosmic Comedy logo—a silver and grey tabby cat with glowing red lasers shooting out of each eye. "Take one of these, too," he urged, extending it in my direction. I took it from him, inexplicably touched by his desire to bestow these small gifts upon me.

Guy-At-The-Table launched into the same well-practiced orientation he had given the group in front of me.

"...If you have any questions, if you have any queries, just come back here and talk to me," he instructed. "When you're ready, go ahead and seat yourself in the main section. Feel free to sit next to people, talk to people."

I winced at this. I had my strengths, but the ability to casually mingle with strangers was not one of them. Guy-At-The-Table craned his neck in the direction of the main space and then turned back to me.

"There's plenty of room, so please take a seat up front. Fill in the empty spaces in the first few rows and all that."

I nodded agreeably, knowing that there was zero chance I was going to sit up front. In fact, I intended to put myself somewhere that offered the most direct means of escape should the evening turn into a snarky heckle-fest, which I fully expected it would.

"How late does the show go?" I asked Guy-At-The-Table. I was thinking about the screaming man, who might or might not be still outside on the sidewalk when it was time to head home. Before he could answer, I quickly explained, "My hotel is about a mile away." And then, feeling chagrined but pushing on, "Will it be safe for me to walk back alone?"

At this, Guy-At-The-Table laughed. It was an easy, kind laugh. Barely hesitating, he flipped his hand at me in a fu-geh-da-bout-it! gesture and said, in a voice that could have convinced me all was right with the world and would be forevermore, "Oh yeah, mate! No worries about that. Berlin is safe as houses."

Once again, his response startled me. One gets used to moving through the world with an assumption of danger and in constant anticipation of crisis. To be told one need not worry at all... There was a nanosecond of pause in which I stared at Guy-At-The-Table, waiting for him to follow this statement with a caveat or qualifier—something like, "But if you feel better about it we can get you a cab...." However, he said nothing more, simply looked back at me with the same unhurried, unconcerned expression.

Feeling oddly flustered at this, I stuttered an awkward "thank you," and turned in the direction of the club's main space. Beyond the entranceway was an open area of about 2,400 square feet with a recessed "pit" in the center containing approximately sixty white folding chairs. The pit was accessible from the main floor by two short, three-step staircases located on either side of the room. At the back of the pit sat a small stage. Thick strands of white tube lighting hung behind each of the gauzy, crimson-colored curtains, giving the stage the appearance of being on fire. Goofy, shiny silver lettering spelled out the name "Cosmic Comedy" on its black backdrop.

In the middle of the stage stood a dressmaker's dummy, clad in a bright blue Cosmic Comedy T-shirt. The microphone perched on the stand directly in front of it seemed to mock the headless dummy, which, being all torso, could never speak its truth.

Dozens of women and men milled around, flowing in and out of the bathrooms, lining up for drinks at the small bar located just behind the stage. A small group of dark-haired twenty-somethings climbed up onto the raised platform in the back, speaking rapidly to one another in Brazilian Portuguese. A few seats over, a very tall woman chattered loudly into her cell phone in staccato French.

I had forgotten what a big international party Europe was. So different from the New England town from which I came.

Watching as others mingled happily together, a familiar rise of shyness took hold. I located a seat toward the back and pulled out my cell phone, scrolling through it manically, as if to indicate that I had extremely urgent matters to attend to before the show started. Knowing that no one was watching, and, yet, at the same time, hoping that my aloneness would not be so glaring as I imagined it to be.

A few minutes later, a male voice penetrated the low, humming babble of conversation.

"PIZZAAAA! HELP YOURSELVES!" shouted the voice, which turned out to belong to the ginger-haired man whom I'd met outside earlier. There was a ragged scraping of metal against concrete as those sitting in the pit pushed their chairs backward, making their way to the upper level where a half dozen large pizza boxes sat on a rectangular folding table. The savory, greasy smell of steaming cheese and marinara sauce penetrated the air. While the scent made my stomach rumble, I remained in my seat. I had been trying to eat healthy lately. I sat back and watched as audience members held the lids of the pizza boxes open for one another, shining their cell phone flashlights inside to identify toppings and make selections accordingly. Hands reached in and grabbed the floppy slices until, eventually, the previously echoing din of multi-lingual conversation was replaced by muffled chewing.

***

A few minutes past nine o'clock, Guy-At-The-Table—now Guy-From-The-Table—bounced up the short set of stairs onto the stage. The overhead lights warmed his skin, turning it golden. Guy-From-The-Table grabbed the mic off its stand and scanned the audience.

"Hello everybody!" he called. I tucked my phone back in my bag, grateful to be able to drop the charade of having more important things to do than mingle.

A few scattered cheers rose up from those around me. Unsatisfied with this lukewarm response, Guy-From-The-Table tried again.

"Oh, come on...HELLO, EVERYBODY!"

"HELLO!" they shouted, louder this time. Guy-From-The-Table nodded with approval.

"Welcome to Cosmic Comedy!" he said. "Can everyone take a seat, puleeeasse? That's right, come on back to the main arena."

Those who were still standing started moving back to their seats.

"Can I get you two there to move one row forward?" Guy-From-The-Table requested of a couple who had just wandered in. "You see, the host is a bit of a prima donna. If he sees these gaps in the audience, he gets all diva-ish and starts having a go at me." He raised his hands, palms up, and offered an apologetic shrug as if to say, Don't shoot the messenger.

I shrunk down in my seat, aiming to make myself as small as possible so as to avoid his gaze. Either I was far enough back that Guy-From-The-Table didn't notice me or he did notice me but could read my determination to stay exactly where I was, for his waving hands fluttered over me to another part of the pit.

"Right!" he exclaimed once not a single gap or empty space remained across the first six rows. "The next thing I need you to do is to make a fuckload of noise for the host. I don't think his parents hugged him enough when he was a child, so he needs our love. Lots and lots of love." He replaced the microphone on its stand and rubbed his hands together. "Alright then!" he said, his voice speeding up, "Giveitupgiveitupgiveitup! for your host, Dharmander Siiiiiiiiingh!"

He raised his long arms skyward in a gesture of exaltation. We in the audience responded obediently with a thunder of clapping, cheering, whistling, and stomping of feet as he grabbed the T-shirt-clad dummy and ran up the stairs to the main floor, disappearing behind the stage. A few seconds later, he reappeared in front of us, holding out his hands, palms up, wiggling his long fingers in a gesture indicating: Give me more, give me more, give...me...more! He allowed our applause to continue for a few more seconds before grabbing the microphone off the stand again. Once our clapping dwindled to a crisp smacking of a half dozen palms, followed by a shuffling silence, he flashed us an amused grin.

"Yeah-yeah," he said, looking pleased with himself. "I'm the host. I'm Dharmander Singh. I'm a tricksy little hobbit, aren't I?"

A burst of approving laughter rippled across the room at this. I joined in. Cute, I thought. Sweet. Nevertheless, I prepared myself for the inevitable heckling that would likely commence at any moment. Dharmander took a small step forward before realizing the microphone cord had somehow become wrapped around his legs. He calmly worked to free himself, unwinding the cord in graceful lassoing loops.

"Goodness!" he said. "What am I doing here? It's like the first time I had sex. Except it lasted longer."

Murmuring laughter from those around me. I marveled at—and slightly envied—how comfortable Dharmander appeared to be standing there under our expectant gazes. Once the microphone cord was coiled obediently next to him, he looked up and nodded again, still wearing the same warm smile.

"So, yeah, I'm your host, Dharmander Singh. Welcome to Cosmic Comedy! If you've been here before, say, 'I have!'"

A smattering of voices around the pit shouted out in unison, "I HAVE!"

Dharmander beamed with what appeared to be sincere delight.

"Welcome back!" he said, leaning toward us affectionately. "We love you! We missed you!"

And then, to the rest of us, "If you've never been here before, say, 'I'm sorry!'"

He said this last bit in a dopey Eeyore voice. The rest of us, mimicking him, called out, "I'M SOOOOORRRRRY!"

Smiling indulgently, Dharmander extended one hand outward, bouncing it up and down as if patting our poor, wayward heads.

"It's alright...don't worry. We love you, too! We're glad you finally made it!" He took a few casual steps across the stage. "But I want to tell you," he continued, "it doesn't matter whether you have been here before or not. By walking through the door tonight, you have...officially...become...part...of...the...Cosmic...Comedy...family."

Someone in the audience whooped. A few more joined in. Enthusiastic clapping followed. I clapped along, though still skeptical, ready to bolt.

"Yeah!" Dharmander said, nodding approvingly. "Everyone here has been adopted. We've all got each other's backs. If someone messes with you, they mess with all of us, right?"

"Yeah!" several people called out, followed by whoops and cheers.

That's nice, I allowed, adding my own vocalization in support of this sentiment.

Dharmander's face morphed into a mock-serious look.

"Now," he said, "let's address the elephant in the room, shall we? I know what you are thinking. Yes, I do. You're looking at me and you're thinking, 'Wait a minute! Wait...a...minute! Isn't that The Door Boy?'"

Busted, I thought, both amused and chagrined. *Guilty as charged, Door Boy...Guy-At-The-Door*...Close enough.

In response to our laughter, Dharmander's face broke into a knowing smile. He nodded eagerly.

"It's true," he said over the waning din of our amusement. "I am The Door Boy. But, you see, I'm from Indian heritage, which means I have to do every fucking job here. Not because I'm a hard worker, but because I'm a cheap bastard. Yeah! But that's also why we give you free pizza!" He gestured toward the cardboard boxes stacked on the table on the upper floor. "We're all a big family, and like an Indian family, we eat together. It's very offensive if you don't eat when you go to an Indian's house. And...pizza! That's very Indian, right?"

Someone in the back let out a high-pitched laugh.

"What?" Dharmander said, holding his hand out, feigning surprise at this. "It's basically naan bread with cheese on it! Fucking Italians taking my culture. Mama mia!"

"Yeah!" another someone shouted out.

"And did everyone get a shot?" Dharmander asked, scanning our faces. An enthusiastic cheer roared to life around me. I stayed silent.

"Yeah, that one's always a bit louder!" Dharmander said with a bobbing nod. "You're all like, 'Yeeeaaaah, we did!' You see, the reason we give you free shots is that Neil, the co-promoter, is from Scotland. And, like a Scottish family, we all do shots together."

Enthusiastic whooping from the audience at this. A man a few rows ahead of me turned his head to his friend next to him and whispered something in his ear. His friend heaved a brief laugh before turning back toward the stage.

"And then...after the show," Dharmander was saying, "we're all going to have sex with each other like...uh...like an Austrian family. We are in a basement, after all. Aren't we, Mr. Fritzl?"

I didn't understand the reference, but the rest of the audience let out a cacophony of groaning laughter.

Looking both pleased and sheepish all at once, Dharmander said, "That's a bit dodgy, isn't it?"

His eyes locked onto a square-headed guy in the front row.

Uh oh. I held my breath. *Here it comes. The inevitable heckling. The cutting remark to let everyone know who's boss.*

Instead, Dharmander offered the man a sympathetic grin.

"Goodness," he said, good naturedly, "you look a bit scared now, mate! Don't worry, we're not one of those types of comedy clubs. Nothing scary is going to happen here. In fact, I have to tell you, because I'm quite proud of this, but we were recently voted 'Friendliest Comedy Club in Europe.'"

My ears perked up at this. Around me, the audience burst into spontaneous applause. Dharmander bowed, then sketched a dainty curtsy.

"Actually," he said, "since we're family now, I have to tell you the truth. When I say, 'We were voted,' what I mean is...me and Neil, the co-promoter, we were getting really drunk the other night, and Neil was like..."

Now Dharmander stumbled around the stage, pointing his finger at an invisible image of himself and shouting in a rough Scottish accent,

"...EH, CUNT!!!"

I chuckled at this, enjoying the irreverence and taking note of the difference between the British use of the word "cunt" compared to its American counterpart. If nothing else, perhaps the evening would provide me with professional food for thought.

Briefly transforming back into himself, Dharmander explained, "Because that's how Scottish people say 'Hello.'" Then, once again as Neil, Dharmander slurred in a booming brogue, "EH, CUNT!!! DO YOU THINK WE ARE THE FRIENDLIEST COMEDY CLUB IN EUROPE?" Straightening up again, he told us, "And I was like, 'Yeah, mate, sure we are.' And he was like, 'LET'S VOTE ON IT!' Because the Scottish...they love to vote. Usually the wrong way."

Laughter.

"So, me and Neil, we voted on it," Dharmander continued. "Put our votes in a hat, checked the results and got...uh...fifty percent of the vote."

Laughter. Dharmander spread his arms out wide, looking exasperated.

"I told you, don't trust a Scotsman with a vote, right? Especially if he's been drinking. So I gave him a hit of MDMA and we voted again. And this time we got 100 percent of the vote!"

Dharmander's charms were starting to have their way with me. I whistled through my teeth again, louder this time, caught by the spirit.

Dharmander responded to our clapping and whooping with another rapid head bob. "That's how democracy works, people! That's how Trump got in! That's how Brexit happened!"

This reference to world events evoked a strange laughter from all of us, one equal parts mirth and moan, amusement and sadness. Dharmander's voice took on a surprisingly serious tone.

"Now, listen, everyone," he said. "I can't believe I have to say this, but please remember...This is a comedy show. You might hear some dodgy shit said up here that you don't agree with, but pleeeeaaaase keep in mind that these are just jokes. What people say on this stage is just to get a laugh. It's not like the President of the United States calling Mexicans 'rapists.'"

Another synchronized, strangled-sounding laugh-moan rippled across the audience. This time it had an even more woeful sound to it, as if it had hitched a ride on the back of a sigh. I found this oddly comforting. My fellow audience members' pained response was a reminder that I was not alone in my dismay at the state of the world.

"Exactly," Dharmander said, giving us a sympathetic half-smile. "So if Donald Trump can say the cunty stuff that he's been saying lately, we should be able to get away with pretty much anything, right?"

The response to this was a sea of whistling followed by a burst of extended applause.

***

The first comedian on stage was a man from Sri Lanka. He had a gorgeous mane of thick, glossy black hair and an equally impressive beard. He flashed us a warm grin.

"Hello...My name is Vidura Rajapaksa. I'm from Sri Lanka, and I'm the brown version of the wizard character in all of your favorite fantasy movies. I'm going for an ethnic Dumbledore, though sometimes people tell me I look a little bit like a chocolate Jesus." He cocked his head and wrinkled his forehead. "That's confusing. Isn't it more like 'historically accurate Jesus'?"

Laughter and clapping. When the room grew more or less silent again, Vidura continued.

"Sometimes just to remind them all, I'll put on my lucky loincloth and head down to my local church and be like..."

He pushed his foot out into the air in front of him as if busting through an invisible door.

"...'Guess who's baaaack!'"

He nodded and said, "The people there are not amused, but I understand. Imagine: The Resurrection, the pinnacle of the whitest religion on earth, and an immigrant took that job, too!"

Laughter and clapping. People hooted their approval.

"I moved to Berlin about a year ago," Vidura said, switching gears. "I finally feel like I'm getting used to the place. A few days back, I was on the U-Bahn and this man got on wearing a full-leather, head-to-toe gimp suit. With bunny ears and a tail. And the first thing I thought was: 'I wonder where he keeps his ticket.'"

I burst out in unself-conscious snort-laughter at the image. I loved sexually irreverent humor—likely a rebellion against the Puritanical New England ethos with which I was raised. After all, doesn't the psyche inevitably seek out balance, attempting to free us from whatever mores once swaddled us but now strangle us?

The tall French woman who had been on her cell phone earlier threw her head back and let out a burst of rapid ha!s at the ceiling.

"I've been dating a lot since I've been here," Vidura told us. "Because, quite frankly, I need material white people can relate to."

"Yeah!" shouted a man behind me.

"Germans girls are more practical than I expected," he said. "This one girl, we got together around December of last year. She broke up with me toward the beginning of summer. Turns out she was just in it for the body heat. I got a little drunk and lonely a few weeks later and sent her a message. She replied, 'Call me back in winter.'"

"And that's not even the worst one!" he told us. "There was this girl, really smart. She was getting her PhD. She used to ask me about my home a lot, about Sri Lanka, about my culture. It was nice! It made me feel kind of special, you know?"

He looked around.

"Until I found out she was writing her thesis in South Asian Studies. I found it, and I read it. And all the stuff I had said was referenced to Native #4!"

At the same time that I laughed, I also squirmed, feeling a wave of guilt by association given anthropology's long, sordid history of the objectification of other human beings. As with many institutions, we were all becoming hyper-vigilant in an attempt to make up for the sins of our professional past. Trying to, anyway.

The good-hearted laughter continued throughout the rest of Vidura's set, some of it coming out in staccato bursts, some in smooth undulations that ebbed and flowed like waves. There were titters and giggles. I even heard a few chuffing guffaws interspersed with deep, throaty cachinnations. All of it together causing the basement to sound as if it had been invaded by a flock of warbling birds.

Vidura's time now up, Dharmander met him at the edge of the platform, giving him a backslapping hug as they passed one another.

"Let's give it up for Vidura!" Dharmander said, waggling his fingers at us in an upward motion. "He's really new at this, so let's all give him a lot of love!"

We were happy to oblige.

***

Toward the end of the first half, a hip-looking young woman with light-blonde hair and glasses ascended the stage.

"Look at me," she said, holding her arms out, "the first woman to perform tonight!"

Enthusiastic clapping. I joined in, feeling another minor wave of guilt for not having previously noticed the gender disparity. For better and for worse—and for everything in between—I wasn't in the habit of making such mental checklists. But it was 2017 and the global #metoo movement had arrived, heralding the beginning of a new, more refined awareness. This was good, this was necessary as we pushed our way up the long, long arc toward justice, but it could also be overwhelming, seeming to require absolute attention and diligence at all times as we kept ourselves on high alert for any and all betrayals of human dignity. Sometimes it felt that there was no opportunity to rest, for what kind of monsters might we become if left to our own self-serving interests?

"My name is Sara Rut and I'm from Iceland," the young woman was saying. "I'm from a place in the far north called Sauðárkrókur, which means 'Sheep River Hook.' Has anyone been to Iceland?"

Several hands thrust up into the air. I considered raising my own, but decided the airport probably didn't count.

"I love talking to people about Iceland," Sara said. "Everyone always asks the same questions, so I'm going to answer them for you now. One: No, we don't believe in elves. 'Elves' is not a religion. It's a conspiracy theory. Two: You don't have to buy tickets to see the Northern Lights. We don't control them, Okay? They're just up there. Three: Because we are only 370,000 people in Iceland, we have an app called *Íslendingabók*. It's to see if you are related to any Icelanders. Because it's better to be safe than sorry! It's so embarrassing to hook up with someone, and then a week later go to a family reunion and see your one-night stand. It's like, 'Oh! We're cousins? Niiiiicccce.' So get the app."

When she left the stage a few minutes later, I discovered the edges of my lips were curved upward in a small smile and a warmth was flooding through my solar plexus. The sensation was surprising, yet distantly familiar, as if something I thought I had lost for good was starting to find its way back to me in tentative increments.

**

Closing out the first half was Carlos del Ritmo from Mexico. His brown eyes scanned the audience.

"It's hard living in Germany," he told us. "It's hard because you have to learn German. It's so different from Spanish, you know? In German, you get to smash two words together and make a whole new word. So you have 'table,' which is *Tisch*, and you have 'lamp,' which is *Lampe*. You put them together and BAM! You have...*Tischlampe*. It was explained to me that the second part of the word is what the thing actually is, and the first part of the word is what the thing is made out of. With this logic, imagine my surprise the first time I went to a German restaurant and on the menu they had *Kinderschnitzel*. Of course, the people I was with said to me, 'Carlos, it's clearly schnitzel meant for children and not made out of children.' But..."

He looked around. "...we are in Germany..."

Pause.

"...and this country does have a history of throwing children into ovens."

I exhaled sharply, the smile dropping off my face and a hot pit welling up in my guts. Apparently, I wasn't alone in my displeasure. Around me, the audience's response was close to feral, with angry grumbling, hisses, and boos. A man shouted out, "Noooooooo!"

Throughout this, Carlos's face remained serene. He raised the hand not holding the microphone, extended it toward us and patted the air as if trying to quell an angry mob.

"Calm down, everyone," he said, lightly. "Don't get weird on me. That was clearly a reference to Hansel and Gretel."

There was a split second of pause and then our previous groans and boos transformed themselves into equal and opposite bursts of hooting and clapping. I let out a forceful exhale on the back of a relieved and delighted laugh. He had played us. He had used our impulse toward outrage against us and we loved it. Were perhaps even grateful for it.

Chapter 4

Hooked on a Feeling:
The High of Joyful Togetherness

Halfway through the evening, there was a seven-minute break, at which point most of my fellow audience members jumped out of their seats, making their way up the short flight of stairs to the main level, from there splitting into three streams that flowed toward the bar, to the bathrooms, and outside for a smoke. I sat in my seat, marveling that I was in a stand-up comedy club and, even more so, that I was actually enjoying myself. And not just enjoying myself but truly feeling good. Lighter than I had been in a long, long time.

Physiologically, at least, this made sense. To a certain degree, stand-up comedy evokes laughter by subtly recreating a fight-or-flight response. As the comedian speaks out a rhythm of words and context, a buildup of tension occurs within our bodies as we await the punch. At the climax of the joke, upon the delivery of the rhetorical resolution, that tension is released, producing an almost drug-like euphoria. So there was that. But not just that. The evening was also provoking a professional curiosity within me. Humor has long been considered notoriously difficult to study cross-culturally, since in order to find something funny, both teller and receiver had to share the intricacies and nuances of overlapping worldviews. And, yet, it seemed to me that, despite the vastly different backgrounds of the people on stage and in the audience, there at Cosmic Comedy, no discernable gap existed between us. The Brazilians sitting on the platform behind me laughed as heartily as the French woman in the row ahead of me. When Karolina Machnicka from Poland got up on stage and quipped, "Before I go on, I need you to know that even though I look chubby, I self-identify as skinny," everyone in the audience (so far as I could tell at least) burst into simultaneous laughter, understanding in an instant exactly what she meant and why it was funny. While I had mixed feelings about social media, it occurred to me that our highly networked world meant that for the first time in history a group of international strangers shared a social vocabulary with which to discuss the various debates shaping our current consciousness as we learned to "be with" one another all over again. Although I had sworn off the delusion of romanticism, I couldn't help but feel that, in the midst of our meme-making, our collective unconscious had wound a little more closely together.

Well, maybe that was what was happening, or maybe it wasn't. Who could say for sure? But it felt like something important was occurring there in that basement space. Ever since Dharmander had stepped on stage—though maybe it had happened the moment each of us descended the stairs into the club—something had joined us in the room. An intangible presence, like a *tulpa* or an *egregore* or some other thought form made manifest. I could almost identify it, but every time I came close, it slipped out of my grasp. Whatever it was, it was vital and alive and eager to inhabit the space along with us. Begging to be brought more firmly into being.

***

When the intermission was up, Dharmander climbed back on stage.

"Did you have a good break?" he asked us.

Shouts of "Yeah!"

"Did you drink some drinks?"

"YEAH!"

"Nice! Did you smoke some good weed?"

The crowd tittered.

"Don't be shy," Dharmander reassured us. "It's practically legal here. Anyway, welcome back to the second half! Are you having fun so far?"

Based on the applause following this question, it was clear we all were. And, yet, the clapping seemed somewhat lighter, more detached, as if a bit of the group's previous vitality had dissipated during the break.

Seeming to sense this, Dharmander told us, "You guys are a gorgeous audience! Let's keep that energy going because…"

His voice trailed off as he glanced furtively in the direction of a group of comedians sitting clustered together on a couch on the upper floor. One of them lifted his hand in a half-hearted wave. Dharmander turned back to us, now speaking in a soft, confidential tone.

"Look," he said in a melodramatic stage whisper, "the other comedians don't like me telling you this, but it's important for you to know that while we look confident, actually, we're quite fragile little people. You see, each of us has a little bird in our soul. And if a comedian comes out here and says, 'Helllooooo!' and you all just stare at him like the Children of the Corn, what happens is...that little bird...in their soul...its neck...just...snaps."

He pressed his raised thumb onto his closed fist, as if snapping the neck of a small bird.

"Ooooooooh nooooo!" a high-pitched voice called out, and, at this, everyone burst into delighted laughter. Dharmander nodded.

"That's dark shit, right? But, yeah, the comedians get really discouraged and they don't stay here and party with us after the show. Instead they walk home...in the rain. And if it's not raining, they pour Club-Mate all over themselves, crying out, 'I deserve this hipster shit!'"

Dharmander mimed pouring a bottle of soda all over himself, then slumped his shoulders forward in a dejected stance.

"The comedian walks home, looking like Charlie Brown..."

"Ha! Charlie Brown!" someone else in the audience chortled in agreement, and I joined him, smiling at the sweetly melancholic image of the modern archetype of the world-weary human attempting to move forward despite the fact that the ground below his feet keeps getting pulled out from under him.

"...and instead of celebrating with their flatmates," Dharmander was saying, "they go directly to their bedroom."

He leaned in toward us again in a conspiratorial gesture that caused me to instinctively push my body forward slightly, as if tethered to an invisible string.

"Now," Dharmander said, "you may not know this, but at comedy school they give us these 'comedy tents' for times when the audience didn't like us. It's our safe space. It's full of pillows and there are pictures of all our comedy heroes up on the walls."

He dropped to his knees and, now wearing a glassy-eyed look of awe and reverence, gazed upward at the imaginary photographs as if in front of someone or something utterly holy.

"Up there are people like Dave Chappelle and Sarah Silverman, Chris Rock, Louie C. Kaaaa...uh..."

Dharmander shot us a look of pure chagrin, as he named the comedian recently accused of sexual harassment. In response, we all emitted a simultaneous vocalization of disgust and dismay at the fall from grace of a comedy icon. Dharmander sighed dramatically and mimed taking the shunned comedian's photo off of the wall. Brightening a bit, he resumed his comedy hero roll call.

"Yeah, but we also have Ali Wong and Bill Cos...uh...."

This prompted another long groan from the rest of us. Dharmander shook his head sadly and once again mimed removing a photo from the comedy tent wall.

"The walls are getting emptier and emptier every day, aren't they?" he sighed. "Well, anyway, we look up at whoever's left, and we beg for their forgiveness for doing a shit show. Then we cut ourselves."

"*Ooowwwweeee!*" someone called out.

"Yikes," I laugh-winced and, at this, the guy sitting to my left laughed and nodded at me.

"Depressing, right?" Dharmander agreed. And then, in a single liquid motion, he moved from his knees to his feet in a surprisingly nimble leap.

"Wow," someone said, almost sighed.

"Yeah!" I called out, blushing at the unexpected volume of my voice.

Dharmander held his long arms out toward us. "But you all are a gorgeous audience, so no one's going home sad tonight, are they?"

"Noooooo!" we shouted.

"That's not going to happen tonight, RIGHT?" he demanded, and in response we offered him the full force of our energy.

"Right!" I shouted out. I was powerless to resist. I didn't want to resist. Watching Dharmander prowl about the stage, with his long black hair and uninhibited grace, it occurred to me that in another time and place, he might have taken on the role of preacher or shaman. Not a soft whisperer of prayers. *Noooooo!* Someone evangelical and feverish who could create the same swell of energy amongst his community members, leading them to shout their devotions to an unseen God. But in this life and context, instead of "Hallelujah!" and "Amen!" those of us sitting in the Cosmic Comedy basement called out things like, "I HAVE!" and "I'M SOOOOORRRRY!" In so many ways, the results were the same: relieving the maddening struggle of the singular self by evoking the energy of the group and giving our individual burdens over to an all-embracing force. But what force was that? My earlier feeling remained that some sort of singularity was indeed being called forth, maybe even liberated, out of our enthusiasm. But, still, I could not name it.

"No, that's not going to happen!" Dharmander called out. "Because you are going to give the comedians so much love! They're going to feel so good that they are going to stay here all night until we kick them the fuck out! And then they're going to moonwalk home!"

Dharmander performed a graceful moonwalk from one side of the stage to the other and back again. I spontaneously clapped my hands together in a child-like display of delight.

"Yeah! And then when they get home, they are going to go into their comedy tents, and they are going to call out to their comedy heroes: 'I ROCKED IT, DAVE CHAPPELLE! I ROCKED IT, SARAH SILVERMAN!' And instead of cutting themselves, they're going to jerk off."

Dharmander put one leg out in front of him and gleefully began making masturbating motions.

"Woo!" I shouted, adding to the delighted clamor with which this gesture was met.

"This is when we get the picture of Louis C.K. back out," Dharmander told us. He mimed picking up one of the discarded photos and pretended to ejaculate onto it. Speaking to the man in the imaginary photo, he said, bitterly, "I asked permission, Louis, so it's not sexual harassment, is it, Louie? *Is it?*"

Howling laughter and clapping at this. A delicious pain radiated through the soft parts of my abdomen. It wasn't just that I found it funny, even though I did. My laughter was part amusement at the image, sure. Even more than that, though, it was the relief at the rising sense of being in a place of strength and safety for all. As if under the humorous words and his quick-stroke hand gestures Dharmander was saying: *We here at Cosmic Comedy see you. We see the old monsters and the new monsters of the world, too. You are in our care, and we will make sure nothing harms you.* It hadn't occurred to me how much the recent trauma and dramas of the world had infused themselves into my being—into my muscles and ligaments and everything else keeping my body standing upright. As if with every news story covering the latest betrayal of human against human—the school shootings, the racist chants now somehow made socially acceptable, each and every woman who stepped forward to remind us that the world was not safe for us to simply *be*—all the delicate energies of my body and mind had twisted and folded painfully upon themselves. But as all those around me clapped and cheered at Dharmander's cutting rebuke and the underlying assurance that such behavior is not acceptable here, the opposite sensation—a sense of peace and relief and relaxed aliveness—dropped over me. There was an unwinding, as if a number of bolts holding me together had been loosened half a turn.

A melting into the moment. I was sure that if the applause had not been so loud, the whole room would have heard the sighing sound of the meat and bones and muscles and tendons of my body gently unlocking their vise-like grip.

Dharmander's masturbating hand slowed, then stopped.

"Alright then!" he said, becoming business-like once again. He pulled a notecard out of the back pocket of his faded jeans and consulted it. "Our next comedian's name is…uh…Petar Petrovski and he is from…uh…Croatia." He put the notecard away and switched the microphone from one hand to the other. "This is his first time on stage, so let's show him lots of love, Okay? Let's giveitup!giveitup!giveitup! for Petar Petrovski!"

A slim, dark-haired man with a closely cropped beard climbed the stage. He fumbled with the microphone, attempting to remove it from the stand, before giving up and letting his hands fall to his sides. He looked at us with a shy expression.

"So, this is supposed to be funny, huh?" he said, once our clapping had ceased. "I lost my sense of humor, so this is why I am here."

To this, I could relate.

"Here's my story," Petar continued. "Since I was born, I knew something was wrong with the world. Like, totally wrong with it. I knew it. Like, it's wrong."

He spreads his arms out wide, as if to encompass the entirety of the world.

"This cannot be right. I was searching for years, asking, 'What's wrong?' And can you believe it is possible to answer that question, the question of what's wrong with the world? This is what I found out."

He dug into his front pocket and pulled out a small object.

"Do you see what this is?" Petar asked us, holding it up. I squinted at it, too far back from the stage to identify it.

"A shell!" someone in the second row called out.

"Yes, it's a shell," Petar agreed. Still holding it up, he traced its tip with his forefinger. "Do you see the spiral? If you open yourself up, you will understand that in nature nothing is outside of the spiral. Including the human body. Including DNA. Everything in existence is on the spiral."

He dropped his hand to his side.

"We call it *phi*. That is all there is…the spiral. Atoms and electrons are going around, galaxies are spinning, tornadoes are spinning. When waves crash, they are crashing into phi. Everything is an expression of phi force spinning in this universe. But nobody knows about it. Nobody ever taught it at school. The only thing is a spinning force. To be a Mozart, to be a Nikola Tesla is to spin with the phi force. That's why they were special. Because they were phi."

A light tinkle of hesitant, though not unkind, laughter arose from the audience, as if others, like me, were unsure how to respond to this stream of thoughts. Although I was fascinated with the content and poetics of Petar's words, my earlier good feeling was replaced with a nervous anticipation that what had until now been a seamless evening of laughter might be in the process of becoming derailed. I craned my head around to look at Dharmander, expecting to see a grimace or some other expression of panic rising on his face. But Dharmander was leaning casually backward against the metal railing running upward along the short flight of stairs, his arms folded loosely around chest and a serene half-smile pulling up the corners of his mouth.

Thus assured, I turned back toward the stage.

"The only thing that is not in tune with the phi force, with the spiral, is human behavior," Petar was telling us. "Do you know why? Because our hearts are closed. Humans live with closed hearts. And the purpose of the human is to express what is in his heart. That's the point. That's the essence. Do you get it? You see, if I am going to make people laugh, I am going to make them laugh from their hearts. We expect something from each other. But I just want to be me. I just want to be real."

Several people in the audience nodded encouragingly at this. Others seemed to be waiting for it to be over. Dharmander flashed his cell phone light at Petar, as he had done with each of the comedians to signal their time was almost up. The light from his cell phone hit the silver "Cosmic Comedy" lettering on the back of the stage, creating a minor solar flare that glinted and sparkled in the darkness of the basement.

Petar nodded at him.

"So," he told us, "I should go. Back into the spiral."

There was light laughter at this. A wide smile broke open on Petar's previously serious face as he looked around at us.

"Anyway," he said, "That's not comedy...but it is cosmic!"

In the split second in which Petar's surprising punchline dangled in the air, there was an almost tangible discharge of pressure in the room, as if we had all been held under water for longer than our bodies could take, and had been finally allowed up for air. As his words sunk in, everyone in the room—myself included—exploded in a simultaneous release of delight at his sudden, unexpected marriage of context and content. A tsunami of laughter swelled up amongst us, loudly filling the space for several seconds. Seconds that felt like an eternity.

Dharmander met Petar at the edge of the stage and clapped him warmly on the back.

"Let's give it up for Petar Petrovski!" Dharmander called out, and we happily complied. I pounded my hands together over and over again, only partially registering the sharp little zings working their way into my palms. The pain was overshadowed by an unexpected surge of joy inflating my insides, like a rubber balloon quickly filled with warm, tropical air.

***

At the beginning of the film *Wings of Desire*, the angel Damiel writes in his notebook, narrating in his gentle, lilting *Sprechgesang*:

> When the child was a child,
> it didn't know it was a child.
> Everything was full of life
> and all life was one.[1]

As Petar Petrovski left the stage, it finally hit me. All evening at Cosmic Comedy, I had felt infused by some unnamable, intangible thing, but while I could sense it building and could feel its power, I hadn't been able to name it. But as our applause swelled in a wave of energy that refused to break, I finally recognized what it was.

Several years earlier, while working as the managing editor of an anthropology journal, I had written a review of a book by the renowned anthropologist Edith Turner. The book was titled *Communitas: The Anthropology of Collective Joy.* In it, Turner set out to illuminate the cross-cultural experience of what is known in humanistic anthropology as *communitas* or "joyful togetherness." Communitas, Turner explained, is a social phenomenon arising when individuals stumble upon "the best time they've ever had"[2] and in which "the naked unaccommodated human being... link[s] unreservedly with others." [3] Although, etymologically speaking, *communitas* is related to the word "community," the two are not the same thing. While "community" implies a group of individuals with long-term emotional and/or geographic affiliations, communitas is an experience of collective joy often occurring among strangers, one that arises "unexpectedly, like the wind, [warming] people toward their fellow human beings."[4]

---

[1] Wenders, W. (Director). (1987). *Wings of Desire* [Film]. Road Movies Filmproduktion [Production Company], Argos Films [Production Company], Westdeutscher Rundfunk (WDR) [Production Company], Wim Wenders Stiftung [Production Company].

[2] Turner, E. (2012). *Communitas: The anthropology of collective joy.* New York: Palgrave Macmillan, xxii.

[3] Turner, E. (2012). *Communitas: The anthropology of collective joy,* 1.

[4] Turner, E. (2012). *Communitas: The anthropology of collective joy,* 221.

Yes! I thought, as Dharmander called the next comedian to the stage. That's it! Communitas. Joyful togetherness. While each of us inhabiting that room had arrived at the club filled with our individual concerns and the many rising anxieties pertaining to the historical present, with every punch line, twist of phrase, and mirth-filled moment, all the personal and shared distractions we had carried in with us were washed away on a wave of collective joy. At least it had for me, and based on the reactions of those sitting around me I imagined I wasn't alone in this.

As if to underscore this idea, at the end of the night, after the final comedian had left the stage, Dharmander addressed us all one last time, saying, "So, guys, that's the end of the comedy for tonight!"

"AAAAWWWWW!" we called out. I, for one, was truly disappointed that it was over.

"I know," Dharmander said, sympathetically, "You guys have been a great fucking audience! In one way, I'm like, 'Awwww...It's the end of the night!' But in another way I'm like, 'Cool, now I can go get stoned.'"

From somewhere behind me came a yawp of approval.

"Before we go, let's give it up for Neil Numb, the co-promoter!" Dharmander called, at which point Neil (aka "Scottish Smoking Guy") appeared behind him on the upper riser.

"Yaaaaarrrr!" Neil shouted, throwing his arm up in a raised fist, as if in victory. As he disappeared behind the stage again, an adoring smile spread across Dharmander's face.

"Oooooh...I loooove that guy!" he told us. "I do! He's my albino monkey. I found him in the Scottish forest and shaved him down. Brought him back to Berlin."

At this, giddy laughter bubbled past the lump in my throat, as if I had been filled with carbonation, then shaken.

Dharmander paused. Scanned our faces. When he spoke, his earlier seriousness had returned.

"At the moment we've got a bit of a fucked-up world, don't we?" he said.

A rumbling assent at this. I nodded.

"Every time I put on the news, I get really depressed," Dharmander told us. "But whenever I get to Cosmic, as soon as I'm at the door and the first few people walk in, it affects me so positively. Suddenly the world doesn't seem like such a shit place."

"Woo!" someone called out, causing a few more Woo!s to ignite around me. I swallowed back a lump in my throat.

Dharmander continued,

"What each night at Cosmic Comedy proves to me is that it doesn't matter where we're from. It doesn't matter our ages, our political background, our genders, our sexualities, our religion, our color, or whatever. Because no matter who we are or where we come from in this world, we can all sit together for four and a half hours without any fucking problems, eat pizza, do shots...and laugh at dick jokes."

This sudden redirection from the profound to the profane startled us all into another collective peal of euphoric laughter.

"You guys are gorgeous," Dharmander called out over the din. "Give yourselves a round of applause!"

And so we did. The applause was long and lusty, interspersed with cheers, whistles, and the stomping of feet. As I pounded my own shoes on the floor, I felt the long dark shadow of the world leave my heart and mind.

***

Heading back to the hotel that night, I was amazed at the lack of fear I now experienced walking amongst the alien shadows of the city and at the degree to which I felt soothed and lifted for the first time in a long time. This sensation was like a drug for my torn-up, formerly romantic heart, a temporary anodyne against the certainty of doom I had been carrying with me for the past year or more. And, like any drug addict, I wanted more. More of the experience of collective joy. And not only to experience it; I wanted to know more about it—its shapes, its distinguishing features, the circumstances under which it was most likely to be liberated. More specifically, I wanted to understand the phenomenon of communitas as it arose at Cosmic Comedy, and the role Berlin's past and present conditions played in its emergence. There might be no chance of building a perfect world, but perhaps there was still the possibility of finding a perfect place. One that could stand as an example of what might be if we let the better angels of our nature guide us forward.

On my last evening in Berlin, as I sat in an ornate theater waiting for the last of the shows for which I had purchased tickets to begin, I pulled out my cell phone and searched for the Cosmic Comedy contact information. Just before the lights went down, I typed out a quick message asking to speak with Dharmander about a research project I had in mind.

I pressed send. Maybe I'd hear back from him, or maybe I wouldn't. It was in the hands of fate.

The next morning, as I sat at the gate in Tegel Airport waiting to fly home, I found a message waiting in my in-box.

"I got your email," Dharmander wrote. "What's up, mate?"

I couldn't wait to get back to Berlin.

Chapter 5

Do We Really Know It When We See It? "True" versus "False" Communitas

I returned to Berlin two months later, in January 2018, for my first research trip. This would be a fact-finding mission to see whether my envisioned project had legs. I would stay for a little over three weeks, and if all went well, more research trips would follow.

"Couldn't you go when it's warmer?" My mother asked me when I told her I was going back. "Couldn't you go in the springtime?"

I considered this for a moment, then rejected the idea. It seemed to me if I waited more than a couple of months, I ran the risk of losing the thread of this "joyful togetherness" that had arisen at Cosmic Comedy. If I waited too long, the feeling might become a ghost, and why would I ever chase a ghost all the way back to Berlin?

"Nope," I told her. "January is perfect."

Besides, I've always believed winter is the best time of year to get to know a city. In the same way a family does not reveal itself until company has left, until outside eyes are no longer there to peep and judge, most places do not become fully themselves until the fair-weather tourists have returned home, until those who are genuinely rooted in the environment are left alone to work out the dealings of daily life in relative solitude. I wanted to see Berlin as it truly was, when it was *das Ding an sich*, the thing-in-itself. Of course, in order to actually see something as *das Ding an sich*—disengaged from all human observation and projection—one had to remove oneself, the observer, from the equation as well. But I didn't let this concern me. I was certain I could make it happen. Ever since that day in my childhood living room, when my father bestowed upon me the understanding that we were all alone, that it was up to us to change the world through the power of our collective intellect, it had become my personal and professional mission to step outside my own context and circumstance in order to see the world from the perspective of angels that did not exist.

After I returned home from my October trip, Dharmander and I had scheduled a video chat, in which I explained to him the research project I had in mind—or at least a vague illustration of what it might look like.

"It's just the seed of an idea right now," I told him. "But I was really struck by the sweet, kind vibe of the club, and how much I learned about each comedian's culture through humor. I'd like to return to Berlin and attend a bunch of Cosmic Comedy shows. Interview you and Neil and some of the comedians. See who's who and what's what."

At the time, I imagined this to be a purely intellectual endeavor. I had no clue how personal it would become.

"Sounds great, buddy," Dharmander said on the other side of the screen. "We're happy to have you."

"I'll pay for every show I come to," I told him.

"No way," he responded, and the tone of his voice left no room for argument. "You're part of the Cosmic Comedy family now!"

During an email exchange, Neil offered me the use of an apartment he rented out on the cheap to traveling comedians. The apartment was in Berlin's Neukölln neighborhood, a 20-minute U-Bahn ride from the club. The distance made me nervous. I hadn't yet mastered the U-Bahn. Besides, being an introvert, I never like to stray too far from my fleecy pajamas and a cup of something hot.

"Thanks, but I'll find someplace closer," I told him.

"All good," Neil responded. "Besides, I would most certainly lead you astray."

Reading this, I laughed out loud. Feeling giddy, I typed: "I'M COUNTING ON IT."

I booked myself a room in an inexpensive hotel located about half a mile from the club. It was good to be on the other side of the Spree River. As much as I had enjoyed the relative quiet of Gendarmenmarkt with its grand, historic buildings and those eerie, observing figures gazing down from the rooftops, this section of Mitte brimmed with activity. From the window of my room on the third floor of the hotel, I had a not-yet-fallen angel's view of the bustling, five-way intersection of Rosenthaler Platz and of what Jane Jacobs, in her meditation on the great cities of the world, described as an urban ballet, "composed of movement and change."[1]

Below me, on the far side of Brunnenstraße, two young men wandered into a kebab shop. Inside, a brown-pink round of meat

---

[1] Jacobs, J. (1992). *The death and life of great American cities.* New York: Vintage Books, 50.

twirled lazily on a vertical spindle as a mustached man in a red T-shirt sliced off thick cuts with a large knife. To the west, a storekeeper emerged out of one of the tourist shops. He squinted up at the sky and stuck out a hand, checking for rain or snow, then grabbed a swivel rack of postcards, dragging it inside. A woman wearing a black leather jacket and green knit hat walked by him. In her right hand, she clasped a white paper cup filled with something steaming; in her left, the loop of a thin, black leash attached to a small brown dog. The dog wore a dark-teal parka and looked like a tiny human. It yipped at the squeaking sound the postcard rack made as the shopkeeper dragged it inside. The woman glanced briefly backward before pulling her pup along. Closest to me, on the corner of Weinbergsweg and Torstraße, a tall, almost painfully thin man with a gauze patch over one eye limped out of the *Apotheke* clutching a small white paper bag. Another man, walking quickly toward the U-Bahn station swore and jerked away when their paths nearly collided.

"What time do you guys get to the club?" I had asked Neil and Dharmander in a message earlier that week.

"6pm," Neil wrote.

"7:30," Dharmander replied.

Around 7:20, I headed over to Cosmic Comedy. I wanted to get there before the audience arrived. Despite the biting chill, the atmosphere on the streets was festive. A fragment of Dharmander's opening monologue came to mind: "We are in Berlin, the party capital of the world!" And, indeed, every evening, as the sun went down, so appeared the city's nighttime demimonde. For those who loved the night, darkness signaled the start of a new day. The city's bars and techno clubs became the scene of a thousand heightened moments and experiences.

As *Rolling Stone* journalist Thomas Rogers wrote about Berlin:

> In the past two decades, the city's tradition of sexual permissiveness, lax drug policing and left-wing, anarchist politics blended together to create the most sexually adventurous, unconventional party scene in Europe. The city's historical poverty meant high unemployment and large numbers of people with no reason to wake up early on Monday, fueling the appetite for marathon-length parties and a dislike of

closing times.... [It is,] a fuck-off to the rigid capitalist version of time that is enforced in every other city in the world.[2]

Or, as one of his sources told him, "[Berliners are] truly saying that money is of secondary importance, that it's the experience that matters."[3]

I liked this and whole-heartedly endorsed the belief that experience mattered more than any tangible thing emerging out of it. As it turned out, the reality of many Berliners' lack of interest in having a full-time job turned out to be a regular source of comedic material at Cosmic Comedy.

"I haven't really figured out what to do here yet," Henning Wechsler, a German comedian, told those of us in the audience one night. "Like ninety-nine percent of all Berliners. Of course, I have thoughts. I have ideas. As you say in Berlin, 'I've got projects up my pipeline.' For example, I could start knitting organic cupcakes in a vegan cat café. Or maybe become a feminist filmmaker—porn, but not with humans. Alien porn. And they're not allowed to touch, only mind sex. I have no idea what that means, but I'll get a stipend for it. And if the porn career doesn't work out, then I'll finally listen to my inner calling and become a vegan DJ in the *Gemüse*-darkroom at the *Bio-späti*."

I laughed out loud, both at the absurdity of this and what it implied. Berlin, more than any other city I had ever come to know, offered an infinity of ways to *become*. Eavesdropping one night at the club, I overheard one of the comedians, an American, telling his friend that in Berlin no one judged him for not having his life figured out since, "Everyone else here is mostly trying to figure out their own."

Hearing him say this, I was filled with a warm feeling of kinship that was both motherly and sisterly. I wanted to turn around and urge him not to be bullied into becoming one thing or the other. Not before he was ready and only on his own terms.

This dedication to life as a grand experiment was one of the reasons Germany's capital had, over the last eight years, emerged as both one of Europe's most vital and vibrant stand-up comedy scenes and a training ground for aspiring comics.

---

[2] Rogers, T. (2014, February 6). Berghain: The secretive, sex-fueled world of techno's coolest club." *Rolling Stone.* https://www.rollingstone.com/music/news/berghain-the-secretive-sex-fueled-world-of-technos-coolest-club-20140206

[3] Rogers, T. (2014, February 6). Berghain: The secretive, sex-fueled world of techno's coolest club."

"Early on, we had an idea about building a comedy university," Neil would later tell me. "The idea was that you could come to Berlin for three months and we'd send you away with a solid 20-minute set. Fast forward eight years, and today Berlin is the place to go if you want to learn stand-up comedy. It's easy to get stage time, so you can do ten shows a week if you feel like it."

"Nice," I said.

"The scene here is fucking great," he said. "Those of us who were here at the beginning got to write the structure of it, which was all about making it friendly and welcoming."

"We're so spoiled," Dharmander interjected. "Because doing stand-up is like boxing. The more time you're in the ring..."

"The more you're getting your face punched..." Neil offered.

"...and the more you're getting knocked down," Dharmander continued.

"The faster you get better," Neil added.

"It's brilliant!" Dharmander exclaimed. "You learn so much more when you get knocked down than when you've won ten fights in the first round. Because the times you get knocked down in stand-up are the times you can look back and go, 'Why didn't they laugh? Why weren't my punch lines working?' That's what the Berlin scene gives you. It gives you the chance to get back on the horse, over and over again."

With this, I flashed back to what my friend back home had said about the way our hometown had lost something of its heart and soul once the forces of the market pushed out those "exploratory venues" in which one could "let loose and explore the boundaries of your personality and be appreciated for it. Not mocked, but appreciated." We needed such places. Places in which to play the fool without being regarded as foolish. Where one is given a welcoming space to express those thoughts once only accessible to eavesdropping angels. From all accounts, the whole city of Berlin was a kind of exploratory venue, and I already had a great desire to protect it, the way one might feel compelled to protect the radiated tortoise or the Sumatran elephant, or some other creature threatened with extinction. If such places as Cosmic Comedy disappeared, we might forget what kindness and support amongst strangers looked like, and turn into feral beasts once and for all.

***

Unlike the trip to the club during my October visit, this time I experienced no fear moving through the dark streets of Berlin on my way to the club. I imagined myself to be an integral part of the city, its past, present, and future. On the south side of Torstraße, I came across a pair of brass plaques embedded in the sidewalk. During the bike tour, Marianne had told us these cobblestone-sized plaques, ubiquitous across Berlin, were called *Stolpersteine* or "stumbling stones," and were part of a project started in the early 1990s as a way of memorializing individuals (mostly Jewish, but also those from other persecuted groups) who had been arrested, deported, then murdered by the Nazis during the Holocaust. The plaques had been placed at the individual's last known place of residence or work, representing one of their last acts of free will. Many of the etchings had been all but erased by the friction of decades' worth of shoes walking over them, but the two at Torstraße 112 were still perfectly readable:

HIER WOHTE	HIER WOHTE
ERIKA HAITNER	META HAITNER
JG. 1927	JG. 1928
DEPORTIERT 29.11.1942	DEPORTIERT 29.11.1942
ERMORDET IN	ERMORDET IN
AUSCHWITZ	AUSCHWITZ

Somewhere in the building across from me, Erika and Meta Haitner—sisters, I presumed—had once lived an existence as real and vibrant as my own, not imagining what horrors awaited them in the future.

"You are always walking with ghosts in Berlin," Marianne had told us. This gave me chills, for it seemed to me that ghosts not only heralded what once was but also what could be waiting for us around Petar Petrovski's spirals, and time's next dark corner.

***

When I arrived at Cosmic Comedy, the club was startlingly quiet. Without the smell of pizza and bodies to enliven it, the air had a stale, used-up odor. The high-topped table was deserted, the standing lamp next to it clicked off. As I made my way farther in to the main space, I could hear a soft clack-clack-clacking coming from behind the stage. I followed the sound to its source.

The soft illumination from the computer screen glowed blue against Neil's rosy-hued face, which was partially hidden by a rippling flop of hair that had come untucked from behind his ear. Unlike Dharmander, whose extroverted intensity radiated outward like a lighthouse beacon, Neil's personality appeared quieter, more reflective, his attention more focused. In the weeks that followed, I would marvel at the way in which, like a bird traveling on an air current or fishes in the deep ocean, he had an almost preternatural ability to sense the most minute shift in the environment and react accordingly—knowing the moment one of the folding chairs was pushed out of alignment, or when the last slice of pizza had been taken from one of the boxes, or when a bottle of beer had tipped under someone's chair. Over the course of any given show night, he was in constant motion, seemingly everywhere at once, attending to a thousand details that might go unnoticed by anyone else.

Hearing me approach, Neil looked up from the computer. "You made it," he said.

I reached into my bag and pulled out a T-shirt embossed with the logo for the Turkish café back home. Tossed it to him.

"I brought you this," I told him. I had one for Dharmander as well. As one of my colleagues once said of doing cross-cultural fieldwork, "Bring gifts, ask simple questions." I had a feeling, though, that none of my questions would be simple.

There was a clanking sound to our left. The bartender for the evening—a lovely twenty-something woman from Finland—appeared out of the back room, hefting a rack of clean highball glasses on one hip. She placed the rack gently onto the bar and grunted slightly as she did a small, stretching backbend. Seeing us, she raised her hand in a wave.

"Want a drink?" Neil asked me. I replied with my usual response to this question, feeling awkward and square.

"I don't really drink," I said.

Neil groaned.

"Not you, too," he said, enigmatically. Before I could ask him to elaborate, he offered: "Cup of tea then? I'll show you where you can put your coat and bag."

He led me to the back room from which the bartender had emerged, and pointed out the electric kettle and tea bags sitting on a long metal table.

"Water's ready. Help yourself."

"Do you need help setting up?" I asked. "I'd like to earn my keep."

He shook his head. "Naw, we've got it down."

I took this as a polite way of saying I'd be in the way. Neil went back to the computer and, after making myself a cup of tea, I sat alone in the empty club, taking in the gestalt of the space.

A few minutes later, the door at the top of the stairs opened and closed, emitting a long, groaning squeak as it did so. This was followed by the rapid patter of feet growing louder with every step until Dharmander emerged from around the corner, bundled up in a thick jacket and grey, woolen hat.

When he saw me, his face brightened. "Hey, mate!" he said. He extended his long, slim arms outward and came in for a hug. Then he looked around and asked, "Where's Yummy Numby?"

I blinked. "Who?"

Dharmander laughed. "Neil. He calls me Singhy Wingy, and I call him Yummy Numby."

I motioned toward the back of the club.

"Great!" Dharmander said. "Do you want a beer?"

I let out an exhale and declined once again.

To this, Dharmander responded with a bright and spreading smile. "Right on, mate!" he exclaimed. "I stopped drinking myself. Two weeks now and not a drop! Cup of tea, then?"

***

A little after eight o'clock, the stale yeastiness of the club was replaced by the warm, musky smell of human bodies coming in from the cold. As usual, Dharmander sat at the table up at the front, his face open, bright, and generous, greeting everyone as they arrived.

"If you have any questions, if you have any queries, you can talk to me or Neil. Otherwise get in there and have fun!" And then, as a new group of audience members approached, "Hello there! How are you doing? You look familiar; were you here last week? It was last night? Oh fuck, I really need to start drinking again. Hahaha! Anyway, welcome back! Have a shot. What? Yeah, yeah, the shots are all the same. They're just in different glasses...like we are as people! Go ahead and sit in the main section. Either join people's rows or sit right behind them. The bathrooms are there. If you have any questions, if you have any queries, you can come talk to me because, as you can probably guess, I like to talk. Haha!"

A couple of the comedians who would be performing that evening wandered in. Dharmander introduced me. "This is Hillary," he told them. "She's an anthropologist."

"An anthropologist?" one of them cracked. "Are you here because Dharmander's jokes are so old?"

It was an easy, stupid quip. I decided I didn't like this guy so much and, after offering him a half-hearted smile, I turned away.

By nine o'clock, the majority of the six dozen white folding chairs in the pit were filled. Most of the men and women gathered there appeared to be in their twenties, with a few here and there in their thirties. But forty and beyond? Not so much. Me, maybe one or two others. A group of men from Lancaster, England, arrived. They spread themselves out across the red vinyl couches directly below me. One said to another in a loud voice, "The next time you are at the bar, you owe me a shot of tequila!" to which his friend responded, "I do whatever I want. I do whatever I want. I...do...whatever...I...*want!*" Another called out: "Is it nine o'clock yet? Is it nine o'clock? Fuck no. It never will be. We've stepped out of time!"

One in their group, a skinny guy with wire-rimmed glasses, wore a blue and white dress that looked as though it had been extracted from the costume closet of *The Sound of Music,* or maybe *Heidi.* While his friends punched and jostled each other, he sat quietly, occasionally tugging at the dress, compulsively scratching the skin just below his knee-high socks. One of his friends called out to him, "Billy! Eh, Billy!" which prompted the rest of them to bust into a loud, chanting, almost ritualistic song, sung so fast that I couldn't make out the words.

"Billy" stared back at them with a blank expression. I wondered what his story was.

Just after 9 pm, Dharmander ascended the stage and, as he had in October, started shuffling audience members around, moving them forward toward the stage.

"Hey, you!" Dharmander called out. "Lancaster Lads! There are two spaces there. Move up, will you? You've got to help me out because the host is a proper prima donna, and if he sees gaps he won't come out."

One of the "Lancaster Lads" pushed his friend in the dress forward. Billy obediently took one of the seats.

Dharmander laughed. "That works! And you there...yes, you. Can you move over one seat so that...yeah, that's right."

And then, after a few more seconds of this, "Alright then! Now that that's taken care of, the next thing you need to do is make a fuckload of noise for the host. I don't think his parents hugged him much..."

Another empty beer bottle clinked against the floor. The Lancaster Lads shoved each other around lightly.

"...unless he thinks this is Wembley Stadium..." Dharmander was saying over the commotion. Hearing their home stadium mentioned, one of the Lancaster Lads let out a drunken hoot. Dharmander swiveled his head in the direction of the voice and said, good naturedly, "Eh! Chill out over there Lancaster! Chill out." Once again speaking to the audience as a whole, "So let's pretend this is Wembley Stadium. Start clapping! Start cheering!"

And so we did. Exactly as he had at the October show, Dharmander grabbed the dressmaker's dummy and ran off the stage with it, disappearing into the shadows.

Watching this opening skit enacted all over again, my heart sank a little. Intellectually, I knew it was ridiculous to be surprised by the repetition. With four shows a week, fifty-two weeks a year, Dharmander could hardly be expected to do a different setup every night. But, still, it caused me to question the premise of my research that had brought me back to Berlin.

In her book on joyful togetherness, Edith Turner made a distinction between "true" and "false" communitas. True communitas, she wrote, is spontaneous and genuine, never forced or constructed. It cannot be packaged and repurposed. It arises out of the organic center of our hearts and minds, or not at all. Human beings, Turner insisted, "have innate knowledge of genuine interactive communitas...we know it all our lives."[4] *But do we really?* I wondered as I watched Dharmander go through these now-familiar motions. Could I trust my judgment when it came to distinguishing between true and false collective joy? Even at that point in my process I had some glimmer of understanding that, due to various factors stemming from both nature and nurture, it was possible that I might be particularly predisposed to being deceived in this way. As the mystic Meister Eckhart said, "When the soul wants to have an experience of something, she throws an image of the thing ahead of her and then enters into it."[5]

Seeing Dharmander run off the stage with the dressmaker's dummy, I was filled with crushing uncertainty and sudden recognition of the possibility that my experience of communitas at the club months earlier—one that had bordered on a kind of religious ecstasy—had been a naïve delusion, nothing more than a product of my own wish for

---

[4] Turner, E. (2012). *Communitas: The anthropology of collective joy.* New York: Palgrave Macmillan, 15.
[5] Turner, E. (2012). *Communitas: The anthropology of collective joy,* 222.

something pure and good and true. *Like my previous conviction that we humans could build a better world*, I thought.

Later, Dharmander would tell me, "The way you make an audience connect with you is to trick them into thinking this is the first time you've ever said something. We are magicians. We're doing magic. The jokes are the spells and the magic is that we create laughter from nothing."

"Magic?" I asked, doubtfully. I equated the word with falseness and trickery.

An embarrassed grin spread across Dharmander's face. "I love magic, so perhaps I'm just trying to make myself feel more important because I want to be a magician, but that's what it is. You've just got to have the right spells. You've got to make sure you've got just the right amount of frog's foot or toad's-fucking-stool."

He closed his eyes and leaned his head back. "God, I love being a comedian!" he purred and, as he did, a melting rapture spread across his face. While in the light I could see the scattered threads of white showing through his predominantly black stubble, the gesture made him appear much younger than his forty-three years.

Indeed, the dismay I experienced as I watched Dharmander re-enact the same opening by rushing off the stage with the dressmaker's dummy was similar to discovering that the disappearing magician's assistant or the bunny rabbit being pulled out of a hat was only an illusion. *Or*, a voice inside me piped up, *like realizing the statues on the rooftops of buildings are not angels. Only statues that will never, ever move.*

For the rest of the audience, however, the illusion of spontaneity was complete. Everyone around me applauded wildly as Dharmander jumped back on the stage. One of the Lancaster Lads shouted out something unintelligible.

"Calm down, Lancaster, ya wanker!" Dharmander said to him. And then, to the rest of us, "I'm from England, so I can talk to them like that."

Laughter from the audience.

"Yes, believe it or not, I am English," Dharmander told us. "I know it's hard to tell because of my sun-kissed skin. When I first moved to Berlin ten years ago, the Germans, they didn't believe I was from England! They'd see me, and they'd be like, *Woher kommst du?* 'Where do you come from?' And I'd be like, *Ich komme aus England.* 'I come from England.' And then they'd give me that weird Scooby-Doo look."

He lowered the microphone and enacted the classic Scooby Doo double take so accurately that I momentarily flashed back to the countless Saturday mornings as a child when my sister and I would park ourselves in front of the television, watching cartoons for hours, eating the oranges my mother had peeled for us, followed by toaster-oven donuts with hot, sticky glaze melting over our fragile fingertips. A delicious pain.

Dharmander continued, "This one German guy, he actually said to me, 'But you do not look English, *ja*?' And even though I knew what he meant, I decided I was going to fuck with him. And so I said, 'Whaddya mean I don't look English, bro? Whaddya want me to do? Drink a cup of tea? Will I be English then? Do you want me to wear a bowler hat? Will I be English then?"

Pointing to the back edge of the stage and looking even more indignant, he added, "Do you want me to go over to that corner and try to colonize it?" He flashed us a naughty smile and nodded. "That'd make me English, right?"

Hearty laughter.

"And this guy was all like, 'Ooooooohhhhhh!'" Dharmander said, jumping up and down. "Because Germans don't like to come across as racist. For some reason. I don't know why."

Now leaning in, speaking to us in a conspiratorial tone, "Actually, I *do* know why. You know why, too, huh?"

A low chuckling. Heads bobbed across the audience.

"So I'm like, 'Whaddya mean, huh? Whaddya mean, huh?'" Dharmander continued. "And the German guy was like, 'Nein! Oh mein Got! What I mean to say is... What is your background, brown man?' And I was like, 'Oh, sorry! We crossed wires! My background is computer science and literature. But don't worry, I'm not here for your job.' And the guy was all like, 'Oh! Oh! Oh!'... You know, freaking out and shit. I finally decided to put him out of his misery and so I said, 'You want to know why I'm brown, yeah?' And he's like, 'Jaaaa!'

"So I explained to him that I am from England, but my parents are from this tiny little country called India. You might have heard of it. And that makes me Indian-English, right? Which makes me multi-cultural."

Dharmander paced across the stage.

"When I first came to Berlin ten years ago, even the term 'multi-cultural' was too fucking racist for some Germans. So they started saying '*Multikulti*' instead. Right? Multi-cultural turned into Multikulti. Multi-fucking-kulti," he repeated slowly, shaking his head. "It sounds like a vitamin drink, doesn't it? Something you'd get at the gym."

He stopped in the middle of the stage.

"Which makes me wonder: If my Indian-Englishness is too much multi-kulti for the Germans, what's going to happen if I have kids? Because my partner, she's German-Polish, which means my kids, if I ever have them, will be Indian-English-German-Polish. They'll be tutti-fruitti-multi-kulti. Sounds like a vegan ice cream flavor, doesn't it?"

As we laughed, Dharmander squinted across the room.

"Hey, Lancaster Frau!" he called, out pointing at the guy in the dress. "What's your name again, buddy?"

I leaned forward, feeling a minor excitement that the mystery of the guy in the Heidi dress might get resolved.

"Billy."

"Billy! So, Billy, you're about to get married, yeah?"

"Yeah!"

"How long have you and your partner been together?"

"Eight years."

"Eight years! No shit, man! Let's give him a round of applause."

Clapping and cheering from the audience.

"That's great," Dharmander continued. "Because, you know, Berlin is not a relationship city. Your average relationship in Berlin lasts...uh...about three U-Bahn stations. You meet. You fuck. You leave."

The laughter filling the room sounded like that of recognition.

"Eight years, huh?" Dharmander said. "Man, you're doing goooood! I, myself, am in an eighteen-year-old relationship."

He paused to let this sink in.

"Now, when I say I'm in an eighteen-year-old relationship, it means I have been going out with the same person for eighteen years, not that I'm going out with an eighteen-year-old. I need to clarify that because I can see some guys in here thinking like, 'Wow, he's living the dream!'"

Yech, I thought, mildly repelled by this, now having to ever-so-slightly restrain my urge to judge. But who or what exactly would I be condemning? Dharmander? His material? Or were they one and the same?

A charmingly sheepish grin spread across Dharmander's face. "My girlfriend hates it when I do that bit," he said, clearly enjoying keeping us teetering on the uncertain edge of mirth and discomfort.

"Actually," Dharmander continued, "she's not just my girlfriend, she's my fiancée."

Cheers of approval. I did a quick scan of the room to see if his girlfriend happened to be there and, if so, if I could identify who she might be.

Dharmander grinned and bobbed his head.

"I know, check me out, right? And she's not just my fiancée, she's my *Schmetterling*. That means 'butterfly.' And she's not just my *Schmetterling*, she's my *Schatz*. That means 'treasure.' And she's not just my *Schatz*, she's my uh...my visa. Perhaps. Possibly. Someday. Depending on what happens with Brexit."

In the midst of this, one of the Lancaster Lads had shouted out something that was unintelligible to me, but which made Dharmander stop and frown. Now looking uncharacteristically peeved, he said to the guy, "Did you say 'she's my "pussy,"' mate? Who are you, Harvey Wank-stein?"

At Dharmander's rebuke, the audience cheered and clapped. I whistled my own approval, appreciating that he had found a way to shut the guy down in a manner that was non-disruptive and yet made it clear that such behavior would not be tolerated. With this, my earlier concerns about the distinction between true and false communitas—along with the question of which of the two was occurring at Cosmic Comedy—receded significantly. Not every moment at Cosmic Comedy was scripted. Yes, there was structure, there was form. Yes, there were certain ritualistic patterns that upheld each evening's performance and moved it from Point A to Point Z. And, yet, as one of the most highly interactive forms of theater, not everything could be planned in advance. Successful stand-up comedy was a continual call and response. During each performance, Dharmander and Neil and all the other comedians were confronted with an unending sequence of unpredictable variables arising out of the immediate moment.

Perhaps this was a big part of the reason the first Cosmic Comedy performance I had attended months earlier had penetrated my neurotic, trembling psyche so much more than any of the experimental theater I had originally come to Berlin to see. While every form of theater represents a dance between structure and spontaneity, tension and release, stand-up comedy pushed this dance of opposites to the max. Every set represented a thrilling tightrope walk between structure and anti-structure, form and improvisation, proclamation and response, self and other.

Just like all of life.

"None of that kind of talk," Dharmander said, admonishing the Lancaster Lad for his "pussy" comment. He did so in a tone of voice that somehow managed to come across as both light hearted and yet left no doubt he was serious in his reprimand. "We are Cosmic Comedy and this is our safe space of happiness. Speaking of which, before I bring out the first comedian, let's go through the rules..."

***

Eight comedians took the stage that evening.

Hungarian comedian Tamas Vamos appeared first.

"The thing about being Hungarian," he told us, "is that when you tell someone where you are from, there are only two reactions. One is: 'Duuuude!' Because being Hungarian in Western Europe is like being from the United States in...well...anywhere in the world." He paused, then said, "I wrote that before Trump got elected, just so you know."

When the laughter and hooting ebbed, Tamas continued, "The second reaction you get from telling people you are from Hungary is, "Oh, are you hungry?" He rolled his eyes, a gesture of exasperation. "Don't say that, okay? I know it might seem funny and creative to you at the time, but it also seemed funny and creative to everyone who said it before you. Plus, our economy is pretty fucked up, so there's a good chance we actually are hungry."

***

A Cambodian man stood in front of us, shifting nervously from foot to foot as he spoke. His thick accent made him hard to follow. All around me, other audience members leaned forward, straining to understand. When his time was up, Dharmander slapped the man gently on the back.

"Come on, folks, he's really new, so let's give him lots of love!"

And so we did, clapping our support of him as though it was what we had been made for.

***

The headliner for that evening was American comedian Todd Stuchiner. He was about 4'10" and walked with a slight limp. He looked calm and happy up there under the lights and seemed to savor our expectant faces looking up at him.

"How are you guys doing?" he asked.

Whooping and clapping.

"Alright!" he said. "A little bit about me. I'm from New York..."

"Woo!" we shouted.

"...I'm single..."

"WOO!"

"...and I'm a little person."

Silence. Todd waited a bit, allowing this revelation to sink in.

"Yes, indeed, I am now an 'official' little person," he said matter of factly. "That just happened two years ago. I used to be too tall, but then they changed the guidelines. Now I'm right on the line. And, let me tell you, it is fucking sweeeeet. Because I realized, 'Oh my god! I'm the biggest little person they have!' Now I can fulfill my dream of being a bouncer at a midget bar! I can stand there with mirrored sunglasses and a tattoo on my arm that says, 'Death From Below.'"

This was met with low rumble of amused laughs followed by clapping, whistling.

"I can break up fights, like, 'Eh! Stop this fucking shit! Don't make me come down there!'"

He mimed grabbing someone much shorter than him by the hair and tossing them out the door.

"You'd think that being short I would end up dating other short people. But somehow that never seems to happen. My first girlfriend was 6'1." Which, in centimeters is...uh...one hundred...uh...ninety-five...million centimeters. Or something like that. Sorry, I'm American."

A few snickers at this. I laughed along, definitely self-identifying as a metric-system-dense American.

Todd offered us a small, bemused smile before continuing.

"I think when you're dating someone who is a different size than you, there are certain things you shouldn't do in bed," he said. "I found this out the hard way. We were in bed one night and she said, 'Let's do a 69. I said I wasn't sure about that, but she said, "Come on, it'll be aweeeesooooome!"

He lowered the microphone and held his forehead in his free hand, shaking it back and forth. As he did, a young woman in the third row suddenly and unexpectedly called out,

"You can do it, Todd! We know you can!"

A loud, appreciative ripple of laughter erupted from the rest of us at this moment of unscripted tenderness. Todd's head jerked up. He looked around, startled by the positive heckling.

"Wow, was that my conscience?" he said. This was met with another rolling wave of laughter across the pit.

"Anyway," Todd continued after it had subsided, "I thought, 'My mom told me I can do anything I set my mind to.'"

He pointed at the woman in the third row.

"And, also, that lady over there said so, too."

From somewhere behind the stage came the sound of Neil's easy-to-identify laughter, a staccato of bubblegum gunfire erupting out of him in a series of rapid bursts.

"Long story short," Todd concluded, "it was the worst 69 in the history of 69s. It was more like a 6. On the bright side, her bellybutton...was...very well serviced. Don't judge me. What was I supposed to do?"

With the din of applause splitting my ears, my earlier doubts dropped away. I had been right to come back. This was a good place.

Chapter 6

Even Friendship Requires Foreplay: The Exuberant Joy of "Parallel Beings"

Just before returning that January, I had emailed Marianne, the bike guide, letting her know I would be coming back to Berlin. While I half expected not to hear from her, she responded almost immediately—surprised but happy that I would be returning. We made plans to get together.

The morning that she and I were scheduled to meet, I bundled myself up in my coat and hat and made my way southward toward Friedrichsbrücke, one of several bridges spanning the Spree River. On the first day of my October trip, I had passed over Friedrichsbrücke on my way to the café that several hundred anonymous TripAdvisor users had insisted made the best cappuccino in Berlin. A young woman had been playing guitar on the bridge, singing in a sweet, yearning warble:

> How far do I need to go,
> Over land and over sea,
> Until I'll find out,
> Who I want to be?[1]

When the song ended, several people had thrown money into her case. I only had large bills at the time, and had vowed to return when I had something to give her. After all, what we don't support, we inevitably lose, and there's no crying over the loss of the thing one has helped to kill by inattention. Although I had returned to the bridge several times during the October trip, I hadn't seen her again. And so, with time to spend before meeting Marianne, I wandered back down to Friedrichsbrücke, hoping the singer might be there.

Passing under the S-Bahn trestle, just south of Hackescher Markt, I indeed heard music. This time, however, instead of the soothing lilt of

---

[1] Summer, L. (2019). Over land and sea [Song]. *Over land and sea* [Album]. QFTF.

the busker's melodic voice, the air was filled with the hee-hawing belch of an accordion. On the end of the bridge closest to me, an elderly woman with deeply creviced skin sat on a small stool, pushing and pulling the pleated bellows of the instrument. The wide, toothy smile affixed to her face never shrank or expanded despite the obvious effort the instrument took. I considered moving closer to get a better look at her and maybe even take a photo. But it occurred to me that if I were to gaze at the old woman too long—either with my eyes or with my camera—she might demand something in return. Money, certainly, but maybe something else as well. Something I wasn't willing to give.

And why shouldn't she demand something? In the era of social media and viral videos, we had become a world obsessed with capturing and freezing moments of a life—either our own or someone else's. And in this process, other people had become nothing more than objects of documentation, props in our photo shoots, existing, on some level, only for the benefit of our own legacies. We had become like Sartre's voyeur, treating those on the other side of the keyhole as items of perception, only becoming aware that we had reduced them in this way when the floorboard behind us creaked and we discovered that another Other was likewise observing our actions and reducing us in this way as well.

It seemed to me that the choice to objectify others for our own gain was the very opposite of joyful togetherness. Quoting her husband, anthropologist Victor Turner, Edith Turner noted that during an authentic *communitas* experience "a community is sending a proboscis out of itself, a long arm reaching up high with an eye on the end of it that turns around and looks at itself, fascinated."[2] In contrast, so much of life lately had become not about self-reflection but about self-regard, bringing with it an almost manic concern for the degree to which others were judging the validity of our lives. We resisted objectification, yet somehow craved it as well. Affirmation of our existence appeared to depend upon it.

Case in point: "I just moved to Berlin," Henning Wechsler, the German comedian-cum-aspiring-knitted-cupcake-maker, informed us a few nights later while on stage at Cosmic Comedy. "Originally I am from Leipzig."

His eyes traveled across the room over the sea of faces, scanning for recognition.

---

[2] Turner, E. (2012). *Communitas: The anthropology of collective joy*. New York: Palgrave Macmillan, 23.

"I see a lot of puzzled faces in the audience. Okay, Berliners, Leipzig is also a city. It's beyond the S-Bahn ring. Not Spandau, but just as far. I really liked living in Leipzig. It's a very cool city. It's very down to earth. It's a city without hype. You can still be there without an audience."

Pause. Silence. Henning nodded, as though he had expected this.

"I'll explain it to you this way, Berlin," he said. "It's like having zero Instagram followers, but you still know you exist."

The laughter following this remark had an "ahhhhh!" sound that resembled sighing, or like the wind blowing through the green, moist tree leaves of early spring. The sound was lovely, but haunting.

***

A few hours after my encounter with the accordion player on Friedrichsbrücke, Marianne and I met at a Russian café not far from my hotel. The restaurant had a warm, soupy smell, and looked like the salon of someone's Old World grandmother. A jumbled array of black-and-white framed photos hung from the gold-filigreed wallpaper. While a few of the photos were landscapes—open fields and city scenes—the majority were of people. In one, a smiling woman in a 1930s-style hat peered over the shoulder of an elderly man as he read a newspaper. Farther along the wall hung the grainy image of a couple walking into a church, their arms wrapped tightly around each other. Next to that a man in a soldier's uniform stared solemnly into the camera.

Amidst these faces, Marianne and I slid into one of several booths lining the café. The enormous, oval mirror propped up against the far wall doubled our existence, and that of everything around us. As soon as the hostess dropped the menus on the table and disappeared, I found myself experiencing a welling up of the nervousness I often feel when meeting with someone I don't yet know well. Our previous level of comfort was only a memory, inaccessible for the purposes of The Now. It was easy to forget that even friendship requires foreplay. Still, I wished she and I could dive immediately back to the previous level of resonance that had been, for me at least, a sweet, unexpected magic.

But, then, that was the crux of my issues, wasn't it? For reasons that would eventually become clearer to me the longer I stayed in Berlin, while I mistrusted mergence, I demanded impossible things of it as well.

"Do you come here a lot?" I asked, grasping for something to say. Marianne shook her head.

"Not a lot," she said. "Maybe once a month. I hope you like it."

The sounds of lunchtime filled the air. Spoons clinked against bowls of magenta-colored beet soup. There was a low murmuring hum of conversation, punctuated once in a while by a gasp of delight or dismay, as those around us responded to each other's stories—the funny, the tragic, the perplexing, and so many other adjectives constituting a human life.

"Good for you for coming back to Berlin in the dead of winter," Marianne said. "For most of us it's a long, slow slog to springtime."

"This is my favorite time of year," I told her, feeling a touch of pride in my New England Yankee toughness when it came to winter weather. "The grey, the cold...It feels like the weather this city was made for."

Marianne's eyes brightened at this.

"Yes, I know what you mean," she said. "In any case, if you love Berlin at this time of year, you are a true convert."

Her words left me with a rush of satisfaction and the sense of having been given provisional membership in an inner circle reserved for those who regarded the city with an almost religious zeal. In a city in which ex-pats outnumbered native Germans, it seemed to me that there was no one better to endorse my inclusion than another one of its transplants.

Plucking at my napkin nervously, I asked Marianne about her work. She told me the cold of winter meant fewer tourists, which meant less time on the bike. Other than a guiding assignment here and there, she spent her days writing.

"I'm working on a series of essays about Berlin," she told me, the similarity of our work striking me at once. "I just finished one about this old lady who hangs out on Friedrich's Bridge. I call her 'Gangster Granny.'"

My eyes lit up in recognition.

"Do you mean the woman with the..."

I couldn't come up with the word, so instead I pumped an imaginary accordion back and forth between my hands.

"Yes!" Marianne yelped gleefully, and the two of us burst into a simultaneous fit of laughter and delight, startling the man sitting at the next table. The man gave us the stink eye and turned back to his meal.

"I hate the sound of that god-awful accordion," Marianne said.

"Ooooh but I love it," I said. "It's deliciously creepy."

"It definitely is that," she said, and for some reason this sent us into another round of laughter.

***

"Think of parallel beings," Edith Turner quoted the anthropologist Roy Wagner as saying. "When two of them are together they never stop laughing."[3]

With that, the awkwardness was gone and our conversation became wildly alive. Marianne and I discovered we shared a similar desire to unpack the world, to try to make all the chaos understandable. We also discussed our dissimilar backgrounds—her childhood growing up in an Evangelical Christian family in Cape Town, and my more or less atheistic upbringing on the North Shore of Massachusetts. One of the things I liked most about Marianne was that she was as good a listener as she was a talker. Most people monopolize the conversation. As an introvert, I was often grateful for this, for it let me fall back into the old habit of being on the receiving end of a connection without having to give much of myself in return. With Marianne, however, I had the desire to tell her almost everything without holding back. This can be a dangerous impulse, the sharing of intimacy before it is earned, with its implied promise of mutual nurturance. I knew eventually I would discover if the connection between us was the true and lasting communitas of Turner's "parallel beings." But for the immediate moment, this quick intimacy felt like a soothing balm.

We talked and talked and talked, moving from subject to subject, the conversation flowing back and forth with ease, each of us taking turns listening and then building on what the other had said. Marianne gushed about reading Dostoevsky's *The Brothers Karamazov* for the third time, saying, "You will never read a better argument for both the existence of God and the non-existence of God in a single book, written by a single man, who must have been populated by countless personalities and minds to have produced that complexity in such perfect form. It is as if 'God'—whoever that is—opened this man's brain and poured in all things that are human, all powerful answers, even more powerful questions; the rawness, the complexity, the impossibility of human life, and just kept pouring. Kurt Vonnegut was right—everything you need to know in life is in *The Bros K*."

I brought the cup of tea I had been cradling up to my lips and took a long, slow sip of the warm liquid.

---

[3] Turner, E. (2012). *Communitas: The anthropology of collective joy.* New York: Palgrave Macmillan, 197.

"Apparently, Dostoevsky was a rotten gambler and wretched womanizer," Marianne continued, "but obviously Jesus had plans for him, as my dear mother would say."

Hearing this, my chest heaved in a series of surprised, giggling spasms, at which point the tea I was about to swallow threatened to become painfully misdirected out my nose. Seeing this, Marianne let out a peal of laughter and shoved her napkin at me. Once I had myself under control and somewhat tidied up, we cackled like the old women we might someday become together. The man next to us frowned at us once again.

"So," Marianne said, when the laughter subsided. "You haven't told me what you're doing back in Berlin."

At this, a part of me clenched up. When it came to my creative projects, I tended to hold the details close to the vest for as long as I could. Ideas in the early stages were like seeds and embryos, requiring warm, dark spaces in order to grow, cloistered away from the world's often harsh input. I inhaled deeply, giving myself a moment to decide how much I wanted to reveal.

Perhaps this showed on my face, because Marianne reached over and touched my forearm gently with her hand.

"You don't have to tell me anything at all," she said, and there was sincere understanding in her eyes and tone. "I know how it is when you're at the start of something new. Sometimes it's better to hold it all very close."

And with this simple invitation to talk or not to talk, my reticence fell away. I told her about my quest to understand the contours of joyful togetherness using Cosmic Comedy's ethos of friendliness and kindness as a model for what we could become if we allowed the better angels of our nature to guide us.

Marianne listened as I talked for several minutes, not saying a word, sipping her coffee and nodding slightly from time to time in order to let me know she had boarded my train of thought.

"That's very interesting," she said when I had finished. "I won't get into the irony of coming to Germany to study comedy, as I'm sure you've heard that before," she said, referring to the cultural stereotype that the German people are overly serious. "But lately I've been thinking a lack of a sense of humor might be responsible for the rise of fascism."

Marianne stirred the remainder of her coffee in slow, thoughtful circles, the silver metal of the spoon making gentle plinking sounds as it hit the sides of the glass over and over again.

"For example, Hitler had an absolute hatred of Berlin *Kabaretts*, blaming them for the loss of the war and the decadence of Weimar society. He even accused Kabarett producers and performers of trying to undermine the efforts of the Third Reich."

"And," she continued, "look at your current president. The guy practically has a nervous breakdown after every episode of *Saturday Night Live*."

"Exactly," I said, my head bobbing in agreement. "You should come with me to the club some night." We made plans to meet for dinner and a show the following week.

Outside the restaurant, the last of the day's sunlight draped itself across the objects of the world, causing long shadows to unroll along the pavement. After exchanging a hug, Marianne jumped on her bike, waving back at me as she disappeared into the motor rumble of the intersection at Rosenthaler Straße. I trotted across the street, heading back toward the hotel, feeling a sense of elation about this new friendship. The blasting of car horns and the warble of emergency vehicles enveloped me, becoming the soundtrack to destiny. In that moment, I was certain that, despite all the pain and struggle, everything was right with the world...or could be. I was high on joyful togetherness, my new drug of choice.

Chapter 7

"Maybe I Was the Class Juggler": Communitas and the Risks of Participation

A few hours after Marianne and I parted ways, I made my way over to Cosmic Comedy for the evening's performance. I was still feeling high from our conversation. As drained as I could get being around large groups of people with whom I was forced to interact, exactly the opposite occurred whenever I experienced an intellectual and emotional resonance with another. Such moments of connection always surprised me with their ability to counterbalance the presumption of being fundamentally alone in an imperfect, chaotic world. And why not? We humans are bonding creatures, designed to seek out the warm light of others. Evolutionarily, to be a member of a group is to survive and thrive.

And, yet, at the same time that I craved moments of joyful togetherness and even a kind of psychological mergence with others, another part of me resisted it. I supposed this made sense; several features of my existence had predisposed me in this way. There was my solitary nature. I had wrestled with pros and cons of my introversion long enough to recognize its predetermination, that it was like having blue eyes and brown hair. Sure, I'd fine-tuned my personality over the years in such a way that had led me to become a much more extroverted introvert, but those changes had only been a matter of minor degrees. Spending too much time among a large group of people, I still always ended up feeling like a chicken bone picked clean. That feature of my personality had not budged an inch, no matter how far I pushed myself outward into the social world.

There was also the ethos of my culture of origin and the underlying values with which I had been programmed. While some cultures and subcultures considered one's relationship to the group to be the *sine qua non* of personhood, as an upper-middle class, white, New England American of Protestant descent, I was raised according to a highly individualized social model. I was taught that alienation was a virtue, that one must fight against the influence of the group in order to become a pure Self. In her book, Edith Turner pointed out that the American colonial culture mentality held within it a suspicion of anything resembling communitas, believing that such deep bonding with others constituted a threat to one's individual autonomy.

"The historic root of American individualism came from self-made men," Turner wrote. "[F]actory founders, businessmen, for-profit farmers, and slave owners who had forged the new country and pushed its rapid expansion. So when the idea of communitas was first broached in the twentieth century, it needed time to flower and develop as an acceptable concept."[1]

So, yeah, there was nature and culture influencing my relationship with this state of joyful togetherness. But, along with that there was also personal experience—the ways in which circumstances specific only to me had informed how I saw myself as a being with others.

Certain childhood experiences had lingering repercussions.

***

I was a shy kid. Awkward. In middle school, I had two friends: Margaret and Deena. Both of them were as socially inept as I, but somewhere along the way we found one another. The three of us spent every lunch and recess together playing Uno. At that point in our psychological development, it had not yet occurred to us to reflect on the nature of our friendship, to consider the possibility we were friends by default. That no one else would have us. Why would this occur to us? Back then, our existence was like that of caterpillars in the pupa stage—liquid, unformed, in the process of digesting ourselves within the cocoon of our personal realities. As far as we were concerned, there was always the potential for changing from one thing into something else.

Until one day the multiverse of possibilities collapsed into a bitter singularity.

At the sound of the bell signaling the end of recess, Margaret, Deena, and I, along with the rest of the sixth graders, trooped back inside the classroom. The room had an unsettling odor to it—the sour, decaying smell of old milk and puberty. It was the scent of one thing dying while another thing rose up to take its place. Ms. Little, the social studies teacher, was standing in front of the class, hands on her hips, looking

---

[1] Turner, E. (2012). *Communitas: The anthropology of collective joy*. New York: Palgrave Macmillan, 6.

uncharacteristically enthusiastic. On the blackboard she had drawn three concentric circles—one inside the other inside the other. To me, this looked exactly like the diagram of the solar system that Mr. Jacobs, the science teacher, had used to explain the path of the planets moving around the sun.

But this was social studies and not science class. So this could not be that.

"Take a seat, everyone, "Ms. Little said. "Today we are going to have a lesson in social dynamics."

She grabbed a piece of chalk from the metal lip of the blackboard and held it up in the air.

"I want you to name the most popular boys and girls in this class," she instructed.

A confused silence filled the room, followed by a nervous shuffling as we kids looked at one another. Was she serious? No one spoke. Still with a self-satisfied smile on her face, Ms. Little nodded.

"Go on," she encouraged.

"Mindy!" some brave soul eventually shouted. Upon hearing her name, Mindy, the prettiest girl in class, jumped slightly. The corners of her mouth curled upward as she sank back into her chair.

Ms. Little turned to the blackboard and wrote Mindy's name in the innermost circle, the elliptical orbit closest to the sun if this were a diagram of the solar system, which it wasn't.

"Good," she said, approvingly. "Who else is the most popular?"

Made confident by Ms. Little's praise, other students got into the spirit, started shouting out names. Ms. Little wrote each one on the blackboard until there were seven names squeezed into the innermost circle. The calling out of names dwindled, then stopped.

Ms. Little pointed to the second of the concentric rings.

"Okay," she said, "now tell me the names of the next most popular boys and girls in the class."

A cold wave flooded through my body as it became clear where this exercise was leading. An infinity of possible futures was about to collapse. Unspoken realities were about to be vocalized and, thus, solidified. It occurred to me that I could run from the room and keep running—far away from the grounds of this pristine, white-building campus with its perfectly mown lawns and manicured bushes. Every muscle quivered and contracted, preparing for flight the moment my brain or gut (or wherever the seat of decision making resided) told them to do so. That potentiality, at least, remained open, though even the doorway to that possible future was closing rapidly.

The second ring filled. When the shouting out of names had stopped, the only ones missing from the board were mine, Deena, Margaret, and two boys who occasionally played Uno with us. After quickly consulting her attendance roster, Ms. Little wrote our names rapid-fire in the outermost ring, leaving the five of us to float somewhere near the cold moons of Pluto.

The other students looked at us. But how did they look at us? With pity? With glee? With relief that they had somehow managed to escape our fate? I didn't turn around to see. I was frozen to my seat, afraid that any movement or sign of life would call further attention to me. I'd missed the chance to run, but maybe I could still disappear.

Ms. Little cleared her throat.

"Studies say those of you in here," she tapped her chalk within the boundaries of the innermost ring where Mindy and a few others' names had been placed, "are destined to be leaders in your fields. Good for you!"

Mindy and the others sat up a little straighter.

"Those of you in this ring," Ms. Little continued, poking her finger at the middle ring where the majority of the class had been placed, "are most likely to take drugs."

Huh? I thought.

Deena nudged me, "At least we won't use drugs!" she whispered, and the dumb relief in her voice made me feel more alone than ever.

Are you stupid? I wanted to shout at her. *Who gives a shit about drugs?*

Ms. Little's hand paused dramatically over the final ring.

"As for you five...," Ms. Little began, and the invisible band cinched around my ribs squeezed tighter.

Before Ms. Little could say anything further, a small voice piped up from a nearby desk.

"Ms. Little?"

It was Becky. She was quiet, but tough. A few minutes earlier, her name had been placed in a coveted spot within the second ring of our sixth grade social universe. I found myself unexpectedly agitated by her interruption, for despite my horror and shame at what was going down, I was also desperate to hear Ms. Little's prognostication of what the future held for me. If not world leader or drug addict, then what?

What? I wanted to shout at her. *What will I become?*

"Yes, Becky?" Ms. Little said.

"I want my name put outside the circles," Becky announced in a small but firm voice.

Ms. Little hesitated.

"You...what?"

Louder now, Becky repeated, "I want my name put outside the circles."

Ms. Little regarded her with uncertainty. Clearly the scientific paper she had read had not prepared her for this unexpected variable.

"All right," she said, slowly.

Ms. Little carefully erased Becky's name from the middle circle and, with a click-click-clicking of the chalk, began to rewrite it in the outermost ring, next to mine.

"No!" Becky's tone rang out sharp and clear. The sound of it made me forget my desire to hear Ms. Little's prophesy.

"I want my name put outside...the...whole...thing," she said, enunciating every word with absolute precision.

What is this? I wondered. *Voluntary exile? Who would choose that?*

"Are you sure, Becky?" Ms. Little asked, flustered but trying to sound calm.

"Yes," Becky said, her voice small again.

Ms. Little turned back to the blackboard and smudged away the "B" and "E" of Becky's name with her thumb. Then she wrote the entirety of Becky's name outside the circles. She turned halfway around and looked to Becky for approval.

Becky nodded and sat back in her seat.

With a now-trembling hand, Ms. Little dropped the chalk back into the rim of the blackboard and started chirping about the quiz we would be having later in the week, something about the origins of the Greek city-state, or maybe the use of culinary spices in the ancient world. I wasn't paying attention. My eyes were locked on Becky's name, which was now floating all alone in a mottled grey nebula of smeared white chalk on dark slate. While I envied Becky's guts and strength of will that had managed to derail Ms. Little's demented experiment on us, I was also filled with a great sorrow on her behalf. There was something horrifying about that consummate aloneness.

But then I remembered something Mr. Jacobs had taught us in science class.

"Little is known about what exists beyond our solar system," he said, "but soon we will know a lot more."

Five years earlier, in 1977, NASA had launched two probes, Voyager 1 and Voyager 2. Their mission: to explore deep space and send back data so that we might learn what exists beyond the boundaries of the known universe. Perhaps even to realms where non-existent angels feared to tread. As Ms. Little droned on to our class about either pepper or *poleis*, I realized that floating out there in the chalky abyss, Becky was like the two Voyagers—free from the gravitational force of the social universe and all its predictability. No one could possibly chart her orbital path, not even the behavioral scientists Ms. Little had so gleefully quoted as she read our fates. All possibilities remained open to her. She was like the wild card in Uno. She could be anything she wanted to be.

***

I thought about that day in sixth grade as I made my way over to Cosmic Comedy after meeting Marianne. Like so many things of the past, it all at once seemed so far away and yet so painfully near as well. Rounding the corner onto Rosa-Luxemburg-Straße, the street on which Cosmic Comedy was located, I noticed for the first time that the sidewalks and street were embossed with a series of phrases written or spoken by the writer and communist revolutionary Rosa Luxemburg. On January 15, 1919—exactly ninety-nine years prior to the day that I had returned to Berlin for my first fieldwork trip—government paramilitaries had arrested Luxemburg and her associate, Karl Liebknecht. Just a few days prior to her disappearance, Luxemburg had written an editorial for the newspaper *Die Rote Fahne* expressing her support for a future leadership created by and from the masses.

"Tomorrow the revolution will rise up again," she declared, "...and to your horror it will proclaim with trumpets blazing: I was, I am, I shall be!"[2]

Four months after her abduction, Rosa Luxemburg's body was found floating in the *Landwehrkanal*, a canal running parallel to the Spree.

Once inside Cosmic Comedy, I stowed my jacket in the back room, then returned to the front of the club. Dharmander sat at the high-topped table as usual, checking in a group of audience members who had just arrived. Neil was nowhere to be seen. One of the club's regular comedians, an American expat who went by the handle "Jetset Ty Rone," wandered over and sat down next to me. I didn't have a clue what it took to make it big in the stand-up comedy world, but I was pretty sure that whatever it was Jetset Ty Rone had it. That "it." He was a true shapeshifter, possessing a preternatural ability to slip seamlessly

---

[2] Luxemburg, R. (1919, January 14). Order prevails in Berlin. *Rote Fahne*. https://www.marxists.org/archive/luxemburg/1919/01/14.htm

into various alternate personae with just a subtle change in the inflection of his voice or reshaping of his physicality.

During one of his sets, he would tell those of us in the audience, "I love the drug dealers here in Berlin, man. Friendliest drug dealers in the world! It's amazing. I fucking love them! Anyone here been to Görlitzer Park?"

Several high-pitched hoots pinballed around the room.

"I love it out there, man," Jetset Ty Rone said. "I was walking through the park and this dude jumps out and he's like..."

His eyes widened. His neck and arms became loose in their sockets and expanded outward into the air around him. His ordinarily compact frame seemed to take up twice the space it had before.

"Eh, Bruddah!" he called out in a smooth and easy South African accent. His eyeballs jutted out of their sockets. "Bruddah! Come here! I have the best cocaine!"

Reeling in his eyeballs so that they were resting neatly inside their ocular cavities once again, Jetset Ty Rone told us, "I'm like, 'Nah, man, I'm cool. I'm cool.' But then this dude's like, 'What about for your gehrlfriend?' And I said to him, 'I ain't got no girlfriend!' And he's like, 'Mistah! Do you know why you don't have a gehrrrlfriend? And I said, 'No, man, why don't you tell me.'"

Jetset Ty Rone's eyebrows rose halfway up his forehead. His face took on the expression of someone who knows an unknowable truth. I leaned forward in my seat.

"And he says, 'Because you don't...have...any...cocaine!'"

As we all cackled in response, Jetset Ty Rone lowered the microphone a few inches from his mouth. The right side of his lip curled up slightly as he made a resigned clicking sound with his tongue against his cheek. He raised the mic back up.

"And I said, 'Well, shit...give me a kilo!' 'Cause a dude gets lonely."

For some reason, whenever I ran into Jetset Ty Rone, I had an overwhelming urge to bake him cookies. Who knows why? Maybe that's what happens when you reach a certain age. Instead of physically lusting after handsome young men, you want to watch them eat baked goods.

("Well," Marianne mused when I mentioned this to her later, "this is Berlin. They probably have a nightclub for that.")

"Are you on tonight?" I asked him.

"You know it," he replied. And then, "So when are you going to get up there?"

"On stage, you mean?"

He nodded. I laughed.

"Maybe someday," I told him. "Like when the cloudberries bloom."

Jetset Ty Rone gave me a knowing smirk. "So you mean the 32nd of never? At 26 o'clock?"

"You got it," I said. "I'm going to leave that to you people."

A ghost of a smile crossed his lips. And then that shapeshift took place in front of me. His previously relaxed posture morphed into a pseudo-aggressive stance, one that was all at once obviously feigned, yet unnervingly convincing. He placed his hands on his hips, eyes narrowing dramatically.

"Whaddaya mean 'you people'?" he growled. "Huh? Huuuuuh?"

And although I understood he was joking, I began to blush furiously, experiencing the progressive liberal's worst nightmare of being caught in a politically incorrect faux pas, one that revealed that one is not so "woke" as one so desperately wanted to believe. ("Awake" or "asleep"…what strange binaries we had been reduced to lately. It was not an easy time to be merely human, floating somewhere in the middle of both extremes.)

"Oh shit," I said, laughing at his teasing, but also stammering a little. "I mean…you know…you funny fuckers."

"Alright then," Jetset Ty Rone said, the light and easy smile reappearing on his face as he once again morphed back into himself. "We'll see. We'll see."

***

Later that evening, a twenty-something-year-old woman from the United States took the stage. Her chin-length hair, once black, had been dyed a mix of bright lime green and yellow. A bubble gum-pink woolen hat perched precariously on top of her head, looking as though it were preparing to jump from her head and slink away. She removed the microphone from the stand and calmly regarded us. When she finally spoke, she did so slowly, methodically, her words delivered with a purposely flat affect and monotone voice, pausing between short spurts of words in a deliberate rhythm that was more like the cadence of spoken-word poetry than a typical comedy routine.

I was immediately charmed.

"My name is Stine An," she said, then looked around the audience, as if sizing us up. "And I'm dressed like this because you should dress for the job you want, not the job you have. And I'm pretty sure that…"

Pause.

"...when I grow up..."

Pause.

"...I want to be unemployed..."

Enthusiastic laughter.

"...or maybe a cool dad who doesn't care about gender norms."

Stine placed one finger against the bridge of her teal-rimmed glasses and slowly pushed them back up her nose. She tucked a lock of lime green hair behind her ear and continued. "People say that if you can dream it, you can do it."

Pause.

"But I have discovered that if you can dream it, you can wake up from it screaming."

I loved her style. It was sort of experimental and weird and appealed to the part of me that sought freedom from form and tradition. I decided that Stine was my new artistic crush. I wondered if she'd get a coffee with me sometime.

"Everyone remembers the class clown, right?" she asked.

Several heads across the audience bobbed up and down. Mine included.

"But who remembers the class juggler? I mean, I don't remember the class juggler *at all*. Which makes me wonder sometimes..."

Pause.

"...maybe *I* was the class juggler and I just don't remember it."

I howled at this, once again remembering that day in Ms. Little's sixth grade classroom when I felt I had failed some essential test of personhood. To remember such things and cringe was human. To laugh about them, divine. Instead of ashamed, I felt I was in good company.

"As you can tell by my accent. I am from the United States. But I was originally born in Korea."

Pause.

"And because I wasn't born in the United States, I can't become the President of the United States. Which..."

Pause

"...to be honest with you..."

Pause.

"...takes a lot of the pressure off."

Hearty clapping that went on for several seconds.

"In the United States there are lots of stereotypes about Korean immigrants," Stine continued. "That they own liquor stores, dry cleaners, convenience stores. Which, if you really think about it, are the only stores you need in life. I have an uncle back in the United States who owns a convenience store. The whole concept behind a convenience store is that it's convenient. Right? So that got me thinking...what would an inconvenience store be like? So here are some qualities of an inconvenience store that I want to share with you."

She scratched her head, pushing her pink woolen hat even further upward. It would certainly topple over now, I decided, but it didn't.

"Everything in the store is either a fiber supplement or adult diaper. Which is either really good or really bad, depending on who you are. They are always out of condoms. Whenever they do have condoms, they're the really small kind made for dogs. Every five minutes, the person standing closest to you farts really loudly, and everyone else in the store thinks that it's you."

Laughter. Without cracking a smile, she said, "But it's not you." Pause. "You get stabbed for no reason. The magazine rack is guarded by a tiger. A real, live tiger. There's barbed wire everywhere. Your parents are there to judge all of your purchases. And every time you buy liquor you have to show two forms of ID and wrestle the tiger from the magazine rack."

Pause.

"Which," she said, "is pretty inconvenient, but also kind of thrilling at the same time."

Laughter. Dharmander flashed his cellphone light at her to let her know her time was almost up. She nodded calmly at him.

"Before I go," Stine said, "I want to share a piece of life advice. I read a lot of self-help books because I'm too shy to ask other people for help. This is from the Green Self-Help Movement. It's about saving yourself and the planet at the same time. This particular piece of life advice has helped me get through some dark times. And I hope it helps you get through some dark times as well, while also helping you reduce your carbon footprint."

Her voice took on the stilted, hesitant cadence of someone reading out loud.

"'Some people like to run the bathroom faucet to mask the sound of urination. But why waste water when you can just scream?'"

As we in the audience burst into a burst of uproarious laughter, Stine's previously stony face broke into a smile, allowing us a glimpse into the person beyond the comic persona.

"Thanks so much!" she said and bounced offstage.

**

As it turned out, Stine was from Boston, only a little over an hour's drive from where I lived in the United States. When we eventually got the chance to get together for coffee, I asked her what it was that compelled her to do stand-up.

She said, "For one thing, stand-up comedy has changed my relationship with failure. You can't become a good stand-up comedian unless you go on stage, and going on stage means you always risk bombing. I had to accept that the only way I would get better is if I allowed myself to fail, even though it feels terrible."

"That's so great," I said, and meant it. I admired the comedians for what they did, getting up on stage each night and sending out bits of themselves into the world. In doing so, seeing what might echo back. The sharing of one's stories is a highly intimate act, requiring bravery in the form of a trust that the nuances of the self—one's strengths as well as one's weaknesses—will be met with resonance or at least respect (though as one comedian I spoke to confessed, "The first few times on stage, it's bravery. After that, it's narcissism."). In doing so, there is always the possibility that, just as it is for all of us, our attempts will reveal shortcomings that would prove us to be unworthy of the connection and empathy that we desire.

Better to not try than to try and fail, the Trembling Self thinks, even though it recognizes that such moments of connection and mutual trust are the only thing that keeps us sane and whole. But it's a harsh world. To put any part of the self out there in the way that the comedians did had become akin to throwing out a piece of raw meat in the midst of a pack of rabid wolves.

Stay a narrative island, a voice inside me warned, *and your secret self can never come back to haunt you.*

And, yet, watching the comedians interact with one another on the Berlin scene, it was clear that a camaraderie emerged out of their bravery, and, along with that, a place in the social universe to see and be seen. As Stine told me, "Another good thing about stand-up comedy is that, when you go to major cities it's not too hard to find some kind of open mic or venue where you can automatically find people to hang out with because you have a shared identity of being a comedian."

Interestingly, a few days after our encounter at the club that night, Jetset Ty Rone would tell me something similar. During an email exchange in which we made plans to get together for an interview, he concluded our exchange by saying, "You know, I was thinking. You should mention in your research some shit about how hard it is to meet people and make friends as an expat. Stand-up seems to be one of those ways to bridge that gap. If I wasn't doing stand-up, I wouldn't have any of the friends and connections that I have now. Even if you suck, you still can find pity and friendships with the other comedians. On the Berlin expat page, you have post after post of people whining about how hard it is to meet people. Doing stand-up seems to be a quick and easy way out of that gap. You can just take a class, and you have five minutes of jokes that you can use to break the ice with a bunch of people at once."

Wow, I thought. *Tremendous*. Jetset Ty Rone's comment evoked in me both a joy and an envy of the possibility of such inclusion. With this, I thought once again about my classmate Becky. I wondered if she had ever found her place within the social universe or if she was still floating out there alone, far beyond our known galaxy. As much as I admired her boldness in untethering herself from Ms. Little's twisted experiment, I hoped she had eventually found her way back to the world of others, and was receiving the nourishment that could be found there.

Chapter 8

An Ideal Pair: Communitas and the Union of Opposites

The next day, I took the U-Bahn to Neukölln to visit Dharmander and Neil at Neil's apartment, which doubled as the Cosmic Comedy office. This would be my first interview with them, and I wanted to pick their brains about the ways in which they set up the circumstances for collective joy to be evoked night after night. For my obsessed brain, their answer seemed almost equal to the secrets of the universe itself.

As I stepped onto the brightly lit train car on the U8 line, I clutched my freshly stamped transit ticket in one hand. I had been warned by several people that getting caught by the *Fahrkarte* controllers without a ticket would result a €60 fine and public humiliations galore.

During one of his sets, Dharmander told us, "You'll notice that here in Berlin there aren't any barriers to the subway entrance. Everywhere else I go, London, Vienna, Amsterdam, Paris, they all have barriers that you have to swipe your ticket through to get onto the platform. But here, we don't, because in Berlin, we trust that you will buy your ticket. Because we live...in a land...of trust. Which, of course, means that nobody buys a fucking ticket! So what I do is, if the train comes and it's too crowded, just before the door closes, I pretend I'm one of the *Fahrkarte* controllers and shout, '*Fahrkarte bitte!*' You know, 'Ticket, please!' Half the train screams and jumps off and I get the whole carriage to myself! Haha! So, yeah, watch out for the *Fahrkarte* controllers. One day they'll take your money."

My body gently rocked from side to side as the U8 executed a rapid, buzzing sluice from station to station. Passengers got off and others got on, settling into position and then staring straight ahead with expressionless faces. I had once read about a psychological disorder in which afflicted individuals become convinced that other people are not people at all, but rather emotionless, soulless robots with no inner lives. Glancing at my fellow passengers' blank, inward-looking faces, it occurred to me that it would be easy to confuse a lack of outer affect with a lack of a soul or psyche. But, then, I had only to glance at my own blank expression reflected in the subway car window as it sped through the darkness to know this was not so. If everyone else was a robot, I was as well.

Wim Wenders' angels, of course, know better. They know how much unimaginable life is going on inside each one of us at any given moment. In *Wings of Desire*, Damiel wanders down the aisle of a subway car as it makes its way through the intestines of divided Berlin. The camera pans across the stony faces of the passengers, while multiple voiceovers reveal each character's interior dialogue.

"Maybe she doesn't have the money to see another doctor," a man with a rugged face considers.

"When will you finally pray with your own words and not for life eternal?" a woman with large brown eyes demands of herself.

"Why am I living?" another guy wants to know.

The camera stops, resting on a defeated-looking man sitting hunched in a corner. He has given up on life. He is contemplating self-harm. Damiel sits next to him, squeezes the man's shoulder. He touches his forehead to the man's. The man looks up. The lines of his worried brow soften.

"What's going on?" he wonders, sitting up in his seat. And then, as if experiencing a minor revelation, his face brightens. "I'm still here! If I want it...I can get myself out of it again. I let myself go, but I can drag myself out again."[1]

At the busy Alexanderplatz station, I awoke from the hypnosis of my own hidden thoughts as the alarm signaling the closing doors began its flustered beeping. A very tall man slipped through just before they snapped shut. It was hard not to stare. The man appeared to be in his mid-thirties with a narrow face and high cheekbones framing a sharp, pointed nose and a full-lipped, bow-shaped mouth. He had the look of an over-the-hill runway model, one only recently put out to pasture. What hair I could see was cropped short, while the rest hid under the most ridiculously awesome hat I'd ever seen—a Midway-style peaked cap such as those worn by police officers, but police officers in a world created by Dr. Seuss if Dr. Seuss were on some seriously strong acid. The top of the hat was flat and pancake-shaped, with a diameter about three times larger than any reasonable hat should ever be. It tapered

---

[1] Wenders, W. (Director). (1987). *Wings of Desire* [Film]. Road Movies Filmproduktion [Production Company], Argos Films [Production Company], Westdeutscher Rundfunk (WDR) [Production Company], Wim Wenders Stiftung [Production Company].

into a three-inch band that gripped his head snugly, then flowed downward into a long-lidded visor. Made from a glossy black material, it reflected the overhead lights in tiny nova-like explosions. The rest of the man's 6'3" frame donned a zero-albedo attire of matte black, from the knit scarf around his neck to the tips of his worn leather moto boots. A thick gold band adorned his right ring finger and another on his left. These also twinkled brightly under the lights, as if in defiance of the rest.

Marital status...ambiguous.

Planet of origin...equally so.

Scratch that, I thought. *Planet of origin: Berlin.*

He sat across from me, crossed his legs, and flipped open his book. On the back cover was a photo of a ballerina, sitting in a swan-like pose. Written underneath her image were the words, *"Tanz bewegt uns. Wir bewegen Tanz."* Dance moves us. We are dancing.

I love this city, I thought.

***

I exited the train at the Hermannplatz station in the center of Neukölln, leaving my beautiful seatmate behind. Once part of the American sector of West Berlin, Neukölln had earned the nickname "Little Istanbul," due to its large Turkish population. Over time I would come to learn that most (or at least a large number of) Berlin-based comedians either lived in Neukölln—usually in shared *Wohngemeinschaft* housing—or were indefinitely squatting on someone's Neukölln couch.

I emerged from the U-Bahn station, zipping up my winter jacket and pulling my woolen hat down to just above my eyebrows. Like most urban throughways, the sidewalks and roadway of Kottbusser Dammstraße buzzed with a flurry of kinetic energy. A woman in a dark red apron appeared out of the nearest Späti and shouted at a mustached man who was reaching upward, cleaning a splatter of bird shit off one of the storefront windows. Loose plumes of steam floated up out of their mouths as they called back and forth to one another in a language I didn't recognize, the warm moisture of the inside of their bodies meeting the cold, dry air.

A block later, I took a right onto one of the smaller, tree-lined side streets. It was much quieter here. Unlike Kottbusser Damm, where the shop fronts all abutted one another, here retail spaces were few and far between. I passed an art gallery here and a bakery over there, then a homeopathic doctor's office further along. Like so many places—in

Berlin and across the world—Neukölln was moving steadily along the familiar pathways of gentrification. Many comedians wondered where they would go if—or when—rental prices became too high to afford.

A block or so later, I arrived at the apartment and rang the bell. Neil appeared and I followed him into a small room toward the back. To my amusement, I noticed that the tight, neat ship that Neil ran at the club did not extend to his home office, which was a disheveled mess of crumbled Kleenex, scattered papers, cigarette butts, and various other rejectamenta covering every surface. He sat back down at the desk in one corner and started typing away on the computer. A few minutes later, Dharmander came through the front door, looking as though he had just rolled out of bed.

"That's because I did just roll out of bed, mate!" he told me with a good-natured laugh. He set his bag on a chair in the office and headed toward the kitchen.

He turned back and looked at me.

"Do you want tea?" he asked.

"Please," I replied.

"One tea bag, or two? I always double bag my tea."

"I always say you're a double bagger," Neil growled, and although his tone was unemotional, a small smile twitched on his face.

Dharmander flashed him a wicked grin and I chuckled to myself. I loved watching their dynamic. This was a fine bromance.

"That's right, bro. Especially when you're asleep. That's why you wake up with that haloumi taste in your mouth."

Neil cackled.

"Haloumi?" I asked.

"It's a kind of cheese," Dharmander said, closing his eyes a little at the thought of it. "I loooove it."

After Dharmander disappeared into the next room, I positioned my audio recorder on a nearby table, hit the ON button, and asked Neil what had originally brought him to Berlin.

"The same thing that brings everyone," he said, swiveling around to face me. "Heartbreak. I had just had a spat with a girlfriend. We were splitting up. My friend phoned me in the middle of that, and I was like, 'This is devastating' and he was like, 'Come to Berlin. I've got a job for you.'"

After a few years working in nightclubs and bars, he started producing stand-up shows for the then nascent scene.

"For the first three or four years we were all working for free," he said, reflecting back on that time. "The comedy scene didn't explode as a lot of people describe it. It was a long, hard slog. We literally dragged it from nothing to where it is now. But when I saw the first few shows absolutely jam packed I was like, 'There's something here.'"

A brief clattering came from the next room. I turned my head toward the sound, and then back to Neil.

"You two seem like a good match," I said, tossing my head in the direction of the kitchen. Neil leaned back in his chair and lit up a cigarette. A plume of smoke burst abruptly out of its grassy tip, creating a momentary nimbus that obscured his face, then cleared almost as quickly.

"Yar," he replied. "I swore I would never have another business partner again, but with Dhar it's a perfect balance. He's great with people, and my idea of Heaven is no people. I prefer to lock myself in my studio, make T-shirts, muck about in my underpants..."

I smiled at this, once again felt a sense of kinship with Neil's quiet, self-contained intensity.

"...but give me a computer and a few hours and I can pack a room," he said. "And you give Dhar a pile of flyers, and he can do exactly the same. And when we're both doing the thing we do best, it's a powerful combination."

Dharmander wandered back into the room, catching the tail end of our conversation.

"Neil and I share the same goal," he responded eagerly. "We both want to give people a space where they trust us to have their best interests at heart. And like a marriage, we can turn round and have a go at each other."

He turned to Neil, speaking to him directly. "Remember there was that one time at the beginning when I didn't turn up or I turned up really late and left you to fucking sort it all out? When I finally got there, you were proper pissed off. You were like, 'Buddy! Buddy, man! I thought we were a team and you let me down today.' And I was just like, 'Fuck bro, I'm sorry.' I'm still always late, but when I have to be there, I'll fucking be there and not leave my buddy in the lurch."

"What was your impetus for wanting to make it a friendly space?" I prompted, impatient to get to the heart of my research.

"I hate bullying," Dharmander said after a moment's reflection. "One thing that totally fucks me off is if I see people being bullied. It comes from being a little kid. Not that I was bullied...if anything, I was a bit of a bully as a child. But now my job is to be nice. There are toxic comedy clubs and you get an audience that specifically wants to watch a comedian rip someone over there because they are fat or because they are bald, or because they've got a big nose..."

"That's the opposite of what we are," Neil chimed in. "We purposely try not to be like that. Everything we do at Cosmic Comedy is aimed at getting the audience together as one unit..."

"One happy unit!" Dharmander added brightly.

"Yar," Neil agreed. "That's why we squeeze the audience all in the front. That's why we keep the venue a little bit cold."

"And the pizza, too," Dharmander added. "The timing of the pizza is tactical. They have to be able to finish the pizza, have time for it to settle, digest it. We want the show to start as the carbohydrates are kicking in, because if they've just eaten it and the show starts and they're still digesting it..."

"...that's no good at all!" Neil finished, throwing up his hands. "And it's the same with Dhar repeating the word 'family' at the beginning of the show. It's about getting people to the point at which they feel safe to laugh."

As I sat listening to the two of them rattle off their "formula" for a successful Cosmic Comedy show, I once again found myself contemplating the distinction between "true" and "false" communitas. Of true communitas, Edith Turner wrote, "One is not 'socialized' into it, it is voluntary, spontaneous."[2] Falsely constructed communitas, she continued, is often "prostituted as real communitas, sold and used to feign a situation of sugary cooperation, a process by which institutions employ some 'proven' method to win approval and literally to make money."[3]

Given that, I had to wonder: Did all these "tricks" that Neil and Dharmander employed render the communitas that arose at Cosmic Comedy in any way "false"? Had we all been manipulated, subtly programmed through the repeating of certain phrases and gestures— not to mention the free pizza and shots—into experiencing this sense of joyful togetherness?

I posed this question to Neil and Dharmander, hoping it wouldn't offend them. Hoping even more so that their answer would be one with which I could live happily.

Neil stubbed out his cigarette, jamming the lit end into a cracked china saucer.

---

[2] Turner, E. (2012). *Communitas: The anthropology of collective joy.* New York: Palgrave Macmillan, 21.

[3] Turner, E. (2012). *Communitas: The anthropology of collective joy,* 21.

"There's no manipulation," he told me. "We don't attempt to unify anyone. I mean, yeah, we've thought about the structure, the science behind it, but we just do our bit. We create a safe environment where people can unify themselves."

We create a safe environment where people can unify themselves.

I wrote Neil's final sentence in my notebook in an enthusiastic scrawl and underlined it once, twice, then a third time. It seemed to me that this was key to understanding a vital aspect of communitas—or at least as it arose at Cosmic Comedy: While Neil and Dharmander could create a fertile field for its emergence, they could not force it on us. Ultimately, the choice was ours. Without our willing participation, the Holy Spirit of Collective Joy could not be liberated.

Or, as Edith Turner observed, "You cannot get into the zone [of communitas] through an act of will, you can only prepare the ground for it to happen."[4]

Yes!, I thought, underlining the sentence once again. I was about to ask a follow-up question, when Neil said, in a flat voice,

"Of course, no matter how much we may have worked out the science of bringing people together, any number of things can go wrong. It's when things are going well that you have to double your efforts. It's when you think you're untouchable that you fuck up. That's when the magic stops. And part of our relationship is pushing each other to remember that."

What happens when the magic stops? I wanted to ask, but didn't. The truth was, I didn't want to know the answer. I was not ready for anything to disrupt the beautiful illusion that I had found a perfect place in an imperfect world.

There was a whistling from the next room. Dharmander jumped to his feet.

"Tea's ready!" he announced.

Neil handed him his glass.

"Top me off, Singhy."

***

As I rode the U-8 back to Mitte that afternoon, I was feeling good. Elated even. While I had been in Neil's apartment, a piece of my own personal puzzle had dropped into place.

---

[4] Turner, E. (2012). *Communitas: The anthropology of collective joy*. New York: Palgrave Macmillan, 52.

"Give me a computer and a few hours and I can pack a room," Neil had said. "And you give Dhar a pile of flyers, and he can do exactly the same. And when we're both doing the thing we do best, it's a powerful combination."

Opposites don't always attract, but in this case, it was clear that the two of them together made a complete whole—Dharmander with his gregarious, extroverted energy (unlike me) and Neil with his highly tuned introverted focus (so much more like me). The lighthouse and the laser. As Neil had said, they were a perfect balance, each one filling in the spaces in which the other left off. Together getting shit done. Really, really good shit, as far as I was concerned.

I realized that this was an important reminder and lesson for me: So often over the course of my life I had doubted my own style of participation, feeling I needed to do or be something slightly different than I already was in order to be a "true" social animal. So often, a restless, negating inner voice would often whisper, sometimes even shout, that I should constantly push myself past my comfort zone in order to become a fully participating being. In Berlin, at Cosmic Comedy, that same negating voice had been clamoring. Each night I made the choice that rather than sitting in the pit with the rest of the audience, I would position myself on a bench on the upper floor, taking the bird's eye view. It was where I wanted to be. It was my most natural state—floating above, taking in the room as a whole. But at the same time that this felt personally comfortable and satisfying, I worried that I could not fully understand the depth of collective joy without full immersion in the group.

In a moment of candor, I confessed to Marianne, "Sometimes I worry that I remain too much on the outside of things and am perpetuating my position as an outsider."

Her response was immediate. "But remember," she said, "every society or group has people whose job it is to circle the perimeter, to view from the outside how the parts connect to the whole."

It was a moment of grace for me, realizing that I had bought into a false framework about what being a social animal "looks like." As Marianne said, and as Dharmander and Neil's relationship showed, different forms of participation absolutely must exist within our social universe in order to enact the productive unfolding of the whole.

With this, my thoughts flashed back once again to that horrifying day in Ms. Little's class. Perhaps if Becky had not interrupted her, Ms. Little might have told those of us whose names appeared in the outer circle that—rather than drug addict or world leader—we were the ones most likely to become anthropologists or artists or some other member of the community whose role it was to view the world from the outside in.

Chapter 9

The Politics of Laughing: Joyful for Whom?

Toward the beginning of my second week in Berlin, Marianne and I met for dinner at a Vietnamese restaurant just down the street from Cosmic Comedy. Outside on the sidewalk, a man in a ratty jacket and fingerless gloves played violin, despite the iciness of the evening air.

Marianne was feeling low. Her hometown of Cape Town, South Africa faced an unprecedented drought. The city was fast approaching "Day Zero," the date on which Cape Town officials would be forced to shut off the water supply to homes and businesses. I asked Marianne if her parents could leave town and get away from what I imagined could easily dissolve into anarchy.

She shook her head, exasperated. Her parents weren't worried, she told me. They believed God would save them. At this, she clenched the napkin in her hand and swiped it across the table in front of her, sending a small scattering of sugar granules flying onto the floor. She turned her head toward the busker out on the sidewalk who had just launched into a jaunty tune.

"It's very appropriate that that guy should be out there playing as we talk about this," she said, angrily. "It's like Nero fiddling while Rome burns."

The conversation turned this way and that, finally falling into nostalgia. She and I talked about all things we might do differently if we had the chance to live our lives all over again. Marianne bemoaned the time she felt she had wasted not diving deep into her writing.

"I squandered so much time on other, safer things," she said sadly, as she wound a shimmering snarl of noodles around a pair of black-lacquered chopsticks. "Sometimes I feel very discouraged about that. About a lot of things, actually. I hope that in time I can heal here in Berlin so entirely that I no longer look back at my life in regret. Of course, my simmering rage about the state of the world isn't terribly helpful or healthy.

"Then again," she said, brightening a bit, "my anger is at least working in my favor professionally. I'm getting money stuffed in my pockets like a pole dancer by shouting at my tour groups about how, 'Complacency is not okay! Germany went from book burnings to Auschwitz in ten years! You can't laugh this shit off!'"

I grinned, despite the tragic topic. I adored Marianne's impassioned honesty. As a good New England WASP, I so often kept things buttoned up.

"Honestly," Marianne continued, "I keep expecting people to complain about me, but instead they give me piles of tips. Maybe it speaks to a need people have now, a genuine fear of what's happening and the moral vacuum we are living in with the current crop of cunts who are running the world." After considering this for a beat, she added, "I exclude Angela Merkel from this."

"Of course," I said, my grin growing even wider. Now Marianne was smiling as well.

"Anyway," she said, "As long as I can stay here in Berlin, I believe I will find healing." She exhaled slowly, releasing her next words on the back of that breath like a kind of prayer: "I hope, I hope, I hope."

I clicked my chopsticks at a meatball that was bobbing around my bowl of pho. It slid out from between them and darted away, dunking under the broth and taking cover under a dark, leafy green that was floating on the far side of the bowl.

"I feel that way too sometimes," I told her, putting down my chopsticks and picking up a spoon. "I think it's natural at this stage of life to look back and assess the past in order to determine which direction to move into the future. God knows there are things I wish I'd started earlier or had more confidence in myself to try, regardless of success or failure." And then, after considering this, I added, "Ways in which I wish I had participated more deeply with the world."

The restaurant door opened and closed, letting in a quick burst of chilly air.

"That said," I continued, pulling my sweater more tightly around me, "I find as I'm getting older I'm starting to trust the process more. Trusting that things have their own flow and happen in their own time. When I think that way, I have fewer regrets."

I told Marianne something Dharmander told me during one of our interviews. He said that while at times he wished that he had started his stand-up career earlier in his life, the reality was that for many years Asian comedians were not taken seriously.

"Being a brown comedian 15 years ago was a fucking shit in England," he had told me. "A lot of my set was about being Asian and how it was to be Asian at that time. I had promoters saying to me, 'Look, your Indian stuff might work in Birmingham, but my crowd don't really want to hear that.' And I was like, 'Would you say that to an Irish comedian? Would you say that to a Black comedian?' If I'd started stand-up earlier, I might have become discouraged and quit."

After recounting this to Marianne, I said, somewhat sadly, "Of course, while I'm trusting the process more when it comes to my own choices, trusting the process of the world as a whole is a bit more challenging these days."

Marianne rolled her eyes and groaned in beleaguered agreement. "You, me, and everyone else," she said.

Outside the restaurant, the violinist switched over to a more somber tune—one I almost recognized but couldn't place. I watched as Marianne's corkscrewing curls bounced up and down against the curve of her cheek as she lowered her face toward her plate. A flood of unexpected warmth filled me. Despite the direness of the world as it was, I couldn't help but feel a surge of happiness and gratitude for the moment I was in. I thought about my new friends down the block, getting ready for the show—these drinking, drugging, swearing, farting, shitting, unabashedly profane angels from whom I was learning so much about the contours of collective joy. Despite the seemingly endless looping spiral of our lives and of history as a whole, some things still remained utterly unpredictable. Of all possible futures, I had stumbled into this one, and it was very, very good.

***

After dinner, Marianne and I walked over to Cosmic Comedy. Marianne tried to pay Dharmander the 8€ entrance fee, but, seeing she was with me, he waved us both through. After a stop at the bar, I led her to down to the pit and grabbed seats close to the front. Marianne turned to me and said with a mischievous twinkle in her eyes: "So, do you mind if I whisper snarky comments about the comedians throughout the show?"

I stiffened, feeling a rise of that motherly–sisterly protectiveness toward the comedians followed by a sense of irritation, even slight betrayal, at Marianne's words.

"Actually," I told her, trying to sound casual and unaffected, "Dharmander asks us not to talk during the show. There are lots of new comedians here. When people talk, it throws them off their game."

Marianne wrinkled her nose.

"But isn't part of the process of becoming a comedian learning how to handle hecklers?" she said. "Learning to stand up against the punches and all?"

"That might be true at other clubs," I responded. "But here heckling is on par with trying to teach a toddler how to swim by throwing it into the deep end."

"Huh," Marianne said, clearly unconvinced, and, with this, I had a sinking premonition of how easily things could go bad between us.

***

As if to underscore my point about Neil and Dharmander's desire to support new performers, one of the first comedians of the evening was very, very new. The brightness of the stage lights seemed to startle him, and his eyes briefly narrowed into pained slits as he pulled the mic off its stand, holding it a distance away from him, as if it might grow fangs. He appeared to regain his equilibrium as he looked over the audience.

"Can you hear me?" he asked us. "My name is Alec Rees.[1] I'm from Wales. I'm 41. I have a dog, a wife, and three children and...uh...there's a joke in there somewhere." He put his hand on his hip and looked around.

"Right," he said, "I apologize. This is not going well. I'm going to skip that first joke and jump straight to the next bit. So...okay...I'm a committed atheist and I'm up here to convert every single one of you to atheism."

And then, almost apologetically, "Stay with me, it gets funnier, I promise. Uh...okay...There is no God. I know there is no God because...because...."

He let out an exhale of exasperation and shoved his hand in his front pocket.

"I've fucked this up again," he told us. "This is me dying on stage big time."

Someone in the audience started applauding—the crisp, fleshy sound of two hands clapping. Soon enough, the rest of us joined in.

"Boy, it's nerve-wracking up here!" Alec said brightly, looking sweetly buoyed by our affection. "Okay, let's try this one more time."

He eventually made it to the end...though barely. He handed the microphone off to Dharmander, who called out, "Let's give it up for Alec

---

[1] Name and identifying details changed.

Rees, everyone! That's the first time he has ever done comedy, so let's show him the love!"

Marianne leaned in toward me, "Yikes," she said. "That was painful to watch."

I offered her a thin smile, but did not respond. My eyes flicked back to the stage as Dharmander planted the microphone back in its stand. It made an electronic chuffing sound as he did so. He rubbed his now-free hands together.

"Before I bring out the next comedian," he said, "let's talk more about religion! Are there any religious people here? If you're religious or have ever been religious go 'Woo!'"

Silence, except for the soft sound of shuffling feet. Dharmander held out his arms in a gesture of supplication.

"Honestly, we are the friendliest club in the world and I'm not one of these comedians who's like, 'Are you religious?' And you're like, 'Yeah!' and then I'm like, 'Well, fuck you.' I hate those kinds of comedians. So let's try this again. If you brought up with religion or you are religious now, go, 'WOO!'"

This time, several more scattered hoots echoed from around the pit. Marianne joined them. I stayed silent.

Dharmander looked around, a knowing expression on his face.

"I'll bet there are a few more of you out there, because most people were brought up with a religion," he guessed. "Me, I wasn't brought up with just one religion...not just two religions...but three religions!"

Wow, I thought. *Is it more disorienting to be raised with no God or too many gods? Which is more challenging for the fragile human psyche: to look up and face empty skies or to be caught in a vortex of voices demanding one's moral and contemplative attention?*

"Seriously," Dharmander was saying, as if reading my thoughts. "I'm amazed I'm not still on heroin!"

Marianne leaned over to me. "Did he really used to do heroin?" she whispered.

I shrugged.

Dharmander paced the stage.

"The first religion I was brought up with was Sikhism. Do you guys know Sikhism? If you don't know about it, Sikhism is the religion of the people with the turbans and the beards who aren't being accused of terrorism. Sikhism is actually a really righteous religion. It was created to get rid of the caste system. It was the first religion to have female priests. And they carry knives, so don't fuck with 'em."

Scattered cheers at this.

"So, yeah, I was brought up with Sikhism, but I was also brought up with Hinduism. Do you guys know Hinduism? I call it the Walt Disney on Acid of religions. Those motherfuckers...they ain't got just one god! They ain't got two gods! They've got a whole sticker album full of gods!"

Dharmander's face opened up like the sky after a summer storm. His eyes brightened and he moved toward us to the edge of the stage.

"They've got a monkey god! Yeah, a MONKEY GOD! And he's not just a monkey god, but a fucking warrior monkey god! There's an elephant god, who's not just an elephant, but an elephant with six...fucking...arms!" He stood on one foot, waving his long thin arms in a graceful undulation through the air on either side of him. "And then they've got these blue characters named Rama and Sita, who would get into all kinds of adventures. This was way before *Avatar*, by the way. Thank you, James Cameron, for stealing my culture."

Once our laughter had subsided, he said, "But like most Asians in England, when my dad got a really good job, he moved us away from all the other brown people and he plunked us right in the middle of Whitesville. And then, to make me even more English, to make me fit in, he sent me to a Church of England school."

Several people in the audience groaned. Dharmander's eyes widened and he nodded in mutual sympathy.

"Yeah, I know, like I said, I'm amazed I'm not still on heroin. It was really weird for me, because I went from..." he hunched over, moving around the stage like a monkey, "...a warrior monkey god and..." now waving many imaginary arms, "a bad-ass elephant god..." then holding his palms up in wide-eyed exaltation, "...and from Rama and Sita and #bluelivesmatter..."

Laughter.

"To...*this*." Dharmander stood center stage, feet together, arms spread wide as though pinned to a cross. With a fierce growl, he exclaimed, "'This is your fault, boy! This is your fault! I'm like this because of you! Yes, you, Brown Boy!'" His face softened. "It terrified me! As a kid, I had all these nightmares of Jesus chasing me. And the only way I could get away from him is if I went through a maze or a small door, because he couldn't get through."

Marianne and I burst into unanimous, screeching laughter as Dharmander, arms still splayed out in a "T" shape, enacted trying to get through a door while strapped to a cross.

Dharmander dropped his arms to his sides and gave us a wicked grin. "Yeah, yeah, I'm going to Hell. But...no biggie. I've already been to Newcastle."

***

At intermission, after the rest of the audience scattered to the four winds, Marianne swiveled toward me and said, "I see why you like it here."

I relaxed, pleased she had felt some of the club's magic. The two of us watched Neil as he jumped off the stage and began arranging the white folding chairs back into neat rows. When he was gone, Marianne nodded. "Yes, you definitely have something very interesting to study here."

"Pretty great, right?" I agreed, grinning.

"But, let me ask you," Marianne continued. "Aren't the comedians preaching to the converted, at least when it comes to the social and political commentary? I mean, if my evangelical parents were in the audience tonight they would definitely not walk away feeling any kind of joyful togetherness."

It was a fair question. Despite Dharmander's inspiring coda at the end of each evening, in which he praised our ability as an audience to sit peacefully and laugh together despite our various demographic differences, it seemed to me we were not as diverse a group as all that. We certainly represented a mixed group of cultures, genders, ages, and races. As for sexual preferences and religious backgrounds, it was impossible to tell from scanning the room. But in terms of a diversity of political values? Maybe not so much. Even Dharmander acknowledged as much in one of his sets.

"I know none of you English people here voted for Brexit," he told us, "because it would be kind of stupid to be like, 'Fuck off, Europe, we want nothing to do with you!' and then be like, 'What do you want to do next week?' 'I know, let's go to Europe!'"

During one of our conversations, I asked Dharmander if the audience really was as politically diverse as he suggested.

"Oh yeah," he said. "There are definitely people in the audience who voted for Brexit. There are even people there who voted for Trump. The people who come to our shows have all kinds of different opinions." He paused, then said, "At the same time...you're right...it's not an even split. We don't get a lot of racists coming to a show at Cosmic."

Speaking very broadly, we in the audience were generally not the English who chose Brexit. We tended not to be the Americans who voted in Donald Trump. We were not the Germans who wished to strengthen the voice and political power of the Alternative für Deutschland, Germany's growing far-right political party. And so, even before Marianne raised her question, I had wondered: Does communitas count if the group experiencing it is already "aligned" in their essential ideology? I wasn't sure. On this subject, Edith Turner didn't have much to say.

Marianne had pulled out her smart phone, and was scrolling through it. Her eyes were still affixed to the screen as she said, "In fact, I recently read an article in which the author argues that political comedy makes no difference whatsoever in changing the tide of history."

After a few more seconds of scrolling, she said, "Okay, here it is. He says, 'When the late great Peter Cook opened The Establishment, London's first satirical nightclub, back in 1961, he said its inspiration was 'those wonderful Berlin cabarets which did so much to stop the rise of Hitler and prevent the outbreak of the Second World War.' Of course this was just a joke, but Cook's point was clear. Satire was fun, but it had no power. Thirties Berlin had been full of brilliant satirists, but their humor made no difference.'"[2]

Marianne looked up from her phone.

"What do you think of that?"

It was another good question for which I had no real answer. In the weeks between my October and January trips, I had done a bit of reading that had led me to investigate some of the theories about the relationship between stand-up comedy and social change, I had come across the argument that while political comedy may have socially transformative benefits—for example, challenging the system by pointing to the ways in which the emperor has no clothes—the cathartic, anxiety-relieving nature of political comedy could also be antithetical to social change, causing audience members to feel that by participating in this humorous deconstruction of social reality they had done their part for the revolution.

I recounted this to Marianne. "I think there's truth in that," I told her. "It's easy to think the dial is moving when you're laughing together with other people, sharing the seductive good-mind vibe of collective ideological alignment."

Intermission was almost over. People were moving back to their seats. Feeling the need to finish our conversation on a positive note, I said hurriedly, "But, to get back to your original question about whether

---

[2] Cook, W. (2018, January 18). Have Donald Trump and Brexit killed off the dark art of political satire? *Independent*.

the comedians at Cosmic are preaching to the converted, I don't believe conversion is the point."

"What then?"

"For me, at least, the point is that it gives us all an opportunity to become more educated about one another's reality. I mean, just because we claim to have certain social and political beliefs doesn't mean we fully understand the issues that we give lip service to. I sure don't, anyway. We might have an intellectual understanding of it...the facts and figures and so forth..."

"The data," Marianne interjected.

"Right! But we may not really have a true sense of how these issues affect the day-to-day realities of others. Sitting here, listening to comedians from all over the world talk about their lives has made me much more emotionally invested in the world and in the lives of others in a way I never could have sitting at home binge-watching CNN."

The pit was getting noisier. Marianne leaned forward and cocked her ear at me. "For example?" she asked.

"For example, there's a comedian from Lebanon who performs here regularly. She does this bit about how she used to work in an office that was very German, but her new job is so international that she doesn't feel special anymore. She jokes that on the first day of her new job, her new co-workers asked her, 'How many wars have *you* survived?' To which she responded, 'Just one.' And they tell her, 'Three's the minimum here, bitch."

Marianne threw her head back and laughed. "Wonderful!" she gasped. "But...is that a true story?"

"It doesn't matter," I insisted. "Even if the story isn't absolutely true, it reflects a true reality: that there are people in this world who have experienced multiple wars over the course of a lifetime. Being who I am and coming from where I come from, that kind of lived reality is so far beyond my own experience that I can't imagine it except as the most intellectualized abstraction. But then this real, live, flesh-and-blood individual gets up on stage and shares a small part of what it means to be a member of a society who *has* faced war after war after war, and it compels me to feel what it must be like living in that situation. My whole body becomes invested in that reality, not just my intellect. I experience embodied empathy."

"Okay," Marianne said, nodding agreeably.

I continued, "Or when Dharmander does this bit about how it will be harder for him to stay in Berlin after Brexit, I become much more personally invested in the impact of that political decision because I am invested in him as a friend."

I paused for a moment, thinking about the ways in which we are most inclined to protect those with whom we have established emotional bonds.

"So that's why I say I don't think the point is conversion," I told Marianne, wanting to make her understand that which had become so clear to me. "Stand-up comedy—at least in this particular context—can help us broaden our experience of the world in ways leading to more understanding and compassion. That is where true communitas brings us. And," I said, "in the end, isn't that the opposite of the fascist impulse?"

Marianne was about to respond when Dharmander jumped back on stage.

"All right everyone," he told the commingling crowd. "Puleeeze bring yourselves on back to the main arena..."

***

The first comedian of the second half stepped on the stage. Her long, scarlet-colored hair shimmered under the stage lights.

"My name is Anja Wutej, and I come from a tiny country in central Europe called Slovenia," she told us. "Also known as 'Not-Slovakia.' Also known as 'Where the fuck is that?' If you haven't been there, it's actually a really nice mixture of unspoiled nature and high mountains, beautiful blue lakes, and rivers."

An audience member shouted something out. Anja looked momentarily flustered. "What?"

The guy repeated whatever it was he said.

"Ah!" Anja said. "He speaks Slovenian. Okay...well...anyway, in Slovenia there are a lot of forests and we have a seaside. We have a Karstic region with a lot of underground caves and little dragons living in them."

She paused. "Actually, they are not dragons; they are just kind of pinkish, whitish skin-toned water salamanders that are blind and basically look like penises with legs. But let's call them little dragons. We also have an incredibly corrupt government and an amazingly shitty economy. We have beautiful vineyards with lots of delicious wine, which means we are dealing with about two million unemployed, depressed alcoholics."

Laughter.

"Slovenia is a tiny country where everyone knows everything about everyone and everything. I found that it was getting a bit too small for me, so I was like, you know what, let's move to the big world. So I moved to Berlin. But it's hard to get to know people in this city where nobody gives a fuck about anyone except themselves and their art."

Laughter and applause.

"The thing you need to know about me," Anja continued, "is because I come from an environment where knowing everything about everyone is normal, I grew up to be a very detail-oriented person. Which means when I get to know new people, I want to know everything about them. Especially the things they don't tell me. Things I can find out on Google, Facebook, Instagram, Twitter...or in the Vatican archives."

Laughter.

"So I went to a bar and I met John. John was 45 and he told me right away that he's not a big fan of the Internet because he is afraid of stalkers."

She paused for a split second, then continued, "Well, the thing I do, I don't call it stalking. I call it 'research.' And if you want to be a successful researcher like I am, you need to know some tricks. The first thing you need is the full name of your research subject. How do you do that? Well, the oldest trick in the book is to be like, 'Oh my god, John, you don't look like 45, you look like 35. Nooooo, I don't believe you. Show me your ID!'"

Clapping and hooting at this.

"Of course John is very flattered...and maybe a bit scared...but he shows me his ID and I get his full name: John Portendorfer. The next time he goes to the toilet, I take out my phone and Google him. Nothing. I Facebook him. Nothing. I check on Twitter, Instagram, Myspace, YouTube, Yahoo, High Five, and AltaVista. I even download Internet Explorer for some reason."

She paused again, calmly allowing our laughter to rise, then ebb.

"I find nothing. But since I like challenges, I don't give up so easily. I talk with John some more. He tells me about his hometown and that part of his family still lives there. We talk for about an hour and don't exchange numbers. Which, technically, might mean that John doesn't want to keep in touch with me, but at this point I don't care about John's feelings. I want information about John. I want a picture of John." Pause. "I want to see his little dragon."

Howling laughter.

"So what do I do? First, I buy a paper phonebook of the town he grew up in and I call every Portendorfer I can find pretending to be an old classmate of John's. At some point, somebody refers me to his mother, Margaret Portendorfer. But I don't call Margaret Portendorfer. I analyze her. I find out that Margaret Portendorfer is on Facebook and she is really bad at Candy Crush. And since she has no idea about privacy settings, I can also see all about her twelve friends."

Anja looked out into the space in front of her, speaking to an invisible person.

"Among them, your nieces, John. Your millennial nieces who take pictures of everything and everyone. And so I scroll through their five thousand selfies and find a photo of a Portendorfer family gathering. It's a blurry one, but I can see you in the back, John. It will work as a poster in my room. I get really excited about my research skills."

Pause.

"And then I accidentally press 'Like' on that photo. So I delete my Facebook account and change my identity. I'm moving back to Slovenia next week."

Marianne turned to me. "I think I love her," she said.

***

On our way out of the club that night, Marianne and I scooted past the line, waving goodbye to Dharmander as we did so. He called me back to him.

He said, "Hey, buddy, wait...I have this for you."

Odd coincidence: Several nights earlier, winding down in my hotel room after a show, I had been online, searching for a movie to watch. One of the first titles to pop up in my search for "Berlin films" was a movie called *Berlin Junction*. Twenty seconds into the trailer, Dharmander appeared on the screen, playing the role of the main character's nefarious best friend. I messaged him immediately.

"Dude," I wrote. "You are EVERYWHERE!"

I couldn't view it online, so Dharmander had promised to bring a DVD copy to the next show. As we headed up the stairs and back out onto Rosa-Luxemburg-Straße, Marianne peered at the DVD, curious.

"What's that?"

I told her the story. Her brow furrowed. Still looking at the DVD, she said, "That's sort of amazing, don't you think? That of all the films about Berlin, this one comes up in your search?"

"Yes, I guess it is," I said with a short laugh. "But, to be honest, this whole Berlin experience has been full of odd coincidences."

Marianne nodded as if she understood perfectly.

"Berlin is working its magic on you," she said, and I found I loved the idea that the city itself might be a conscious entity, one conspiring to help me along my way. With the blue U-Bahn sign looming above us, we embraced goodbye. Marianne turned briefly back to throw me a wave before disappearing into the dark throat of the Rosa-Luxemburg-Platz station.

Chapter 10

If There Is a God, It's a Trickster God: A Prelude to a Collapse of Meaning

It was true. Berlin *was* working its magic on me. And, like any new convert, I wanted this magic to encompass the whole world. Later, I would discover that while I was in Berlin that January, researchers at the UK-based Ipsos Mori Social Research Institute concluded a global survey revealing that the majority of individuals surveyed considered their nation to be more divided and less tolerant of outsiders than ten years prior. What's more, one in seven of those polled said they believed that interacting with people from other backgrounds, cultures, or points of view inevitably resulted in conflict.

Perhaps that's what was going on in the rest of the world, but, as far as I was concerned, down in the dark basement womb of Cosmic Comedy, the exact opposite was happening. Each night in that dim room, with the stage curtains a blaze of fiery crimson and the smell of greasy pizza and yeasty beer penetrating the air, dozens of us from radically different backgrounds cheered on the comedians as they transmitted bits and pieces of their lived experiences, jumpstarting our imaginations and our empathy, helping us conceive of who we might have been if we weren't who we already were. During one of our conversations, Neil had told me he wanted Berlin to become a kind of comedy university, and while the above may not have been exactly what he had in mind, I was most definitely getting an education. What did I learn? A little of the German language. Some of its history, too. Most importantly, I was learning something about the inner lives of others: what motivated them, what concerned them, what made them laugh, either out of joy or from nervousness or from discomfort. And while this was not everything when it came to building a better world, I believed it was a start. By the time my second week turned into the third and final one, I was full of optimism that, despite the increasing madness and division of the outside world, we at Cosmic Comedy had discovered the secret sauce for a new and better age. Certainly for myself, I felt I was becoming more worldly, more intelligent, and, above all, more empathetic to the intricacies of being alive on Planet Earth. I had identified my ideal position in time and space for the particular kind of social animal I was and had always been. Filled by the spirit of communitas, I imagined myself to be a goddamn warrior fighting for the soul of the world. And that kind of pure righteousness felt so very, very good.

Of course, it's usually around this point that the forces of existence decide to take one down a peg. Sentient or not, intentionally designed or not, the universe most definitely has a sense of humor. If there ever was a singular, conscious, overarching deity I could believe in, it would be a trickster god, an entity tasked with unleashing an uncomfortable chaos, forcing us to come face to face with the best and the worst parts of ourselves. Compelling us to reconsider our previous notions about the world and our place within it.

In my case, the universe brought me "The Night of the Unruly Swedes."

Chapter 11

The Madness of the Crowd: Communitas's Dark Doppelgänger

On the evening of January 29, Cosmic Comedy was at full capacity. I shifted on the bench's flat, wooden surface, trying to get comfortable, feeling antsy and slightly aggravated, as if a dozen tiny beetles were trying to dig their way under my skin. Despite my continued excitement at being there, I was achingly tired, having never fully gotten over my jet lag. The exhaustion had crept into my already rapidly spinning molecules; hence the buggy, burrowing feeling combined with a raw punchiness that precedes an energetic crash. When Neil called out "PIZZA!" a few minutes earlier, I had jumped in ahead of the crowd, unapologetically grabbing two slices out of the box before retreating to the bench once again.

Earlier that evening, I had been hanging out with Dharmander in the entryway, keeping him company as he checked people in. A Syrian man—a regular audience member at Cosmic Comedy—entered the club, rubbing his cheeks with mitten-covered hands.

"I feel like winter just sat on my face," he informed us. He and I got to talking about my research project, and I told him a little bit about it, in particular my desire to illuminate how stand-up at Cosmic Comedy acted as a cross-cultural communication device, bringing people of different cultures and nationalities closer together.

When I was finished, he pursed his lips together briefly.

"You're treating your subject matter with more respect than it deserves," he pronounced. "Stand-up is the lowest of art forms." His eyes flickered briefly over to the stage, lingering there a moment before drifting back toward me. A small smile illuminated his previously expressionless face. "Still," he said, "it is such a pleasure."

"Is there a comedy scene in Syria?" I asked him, already guessing the answer, but not wanting to presume.

"No," he said. And then, "We're all too busy trying to stay alive."

He excused himself and headed to the bar. Since Dharmander was busy checking people in, I casually drifted away, grabbing my usual spot on the bench overlooking the pit. As I waited for the show to begin, I found myself experiencing a kind of vertigo, a swooning sensation in which everything around me became heightened, more alive. The red of the curtains framing the stage sparkled under the overhead lights. A series of solar flares emanated from the silver lettering on the black backdrop, causing me to wince and close my eyes. Somewhere near the bar, a woman with an Australian accent called out, "Hey Janey!" and as "Janey" passed by, moving toward her friend, the air behind me was filled with a mix of sweet perfume and acrid marijuana smoke, which dragged like comet contrails off the back of her wool jacket. A moment later, Dharmander's bubbling laugh emanated from the front of the club, penetrating the low hum of indecipherable chatter. This was followed by an exclamation of "Yeeeaaah, buddy!"

I thought about what the Syrian man had said. Perhaps I *was* treating the goings-on at Cosmic Comedy with more respect than it deserved, but, still, I was happy to be there. Low art form or not, it *was* such a pleasure.

***

At about quarter to nine, a group of ten or so Swedish businessmen and businesswomen on a corporate retreat entered the club. They pushed and shoved one another with the kind of adolescent glee and manic giddiness that occurs when a group of co-workers are given the opportunity to bust loose from the tight boundaries of office life. Exuding the nervous energy of consensual limitations being jettisoned, retested, and reconfigured. That and, very likely, a whole bunch of cocaine.

As always, we in the audience burst into an obedient crescendo of enthusiastic clapping as Dharmander enacted his usual opening routine and ran off the stage with the dressmaker's dummy. The Swedish businessmen and businesswomen—now spread across the third row—started chanting in rhythmic unison. "Oye! Oye! Oye! Oye! Oye! Oye! Oye!"

"Hello everybody!" Dharmander said in his usual let's-have-fun-tonight-'cause-the-world-may-end-tomorrow voice. "My name is Dharmander Singh and, yes, I am the host. But you Swedish fuckers knew that already, didn't you?"

Hearing themselves referenced, the Swedes let out an animalistic yelp. "AAAEEEYAAAH!"

"Welcome to Cosmic Comedy!" Dharmander continued. "If you're not from Sweden, make some noise."

Loud clapping and cheering from the rest of us. I let out a long whistle.

"Okay, good!" Dharmander said. And then, as if presaging the evening to come, "I'm glad you're all out there because otherwise the Vikings will take over."

Which begat a second burst of "AAAEEEYAAAH!" from the Swedes.

"If you've been to Cosmic Comedy before, say, 'I have!'"

"I HAVE!" a small cluster of us called out. In the pit, the Syrian man I had met earlier raised his hand over his head and called out "Jah!"

Dharmander grinned affectionately. "Welcome back! We missed you! And if you've never been to Cosmic Comedy before, say, 'I'm sorry!'"

Whatever "I'm sorrys" there might have been were drowned out by the Swedes, who let loose an even longer, louder, more frenzied howl. "AAAAAAEEEEEEYYYYAAAAAHHHH!" they shouted. Several of them blew raspberries and waved their long arms in the air.

Dharmander took an involuntary step back in response. "Holy shit," he said, eyes wide. "What's happening here? Is cocaine really cheap in Sweden or something? What the fuck are you all putting in your mouths? Are you passing out Swedish crackers? Is that what's making you all so loaded and crazy?"

When one of the Swedes extended one of whatever it was toward him, Dharmander immediately recoiled. "Nooooo, fucking way, dude!" he said, shaking his palm at them. "I've been told by my mum to never put things in my mouth when the Swedes give them to you. Unless it's a penis, obviously. Yeah, I'm going there."

"AAAAAAEEEEEEYYYYAAAAAHHHH!" the Swedes yelped again with unsettling animation. I stiffened, aggravated by their continued outbursts, which, in my mental state, felt like broken glass scraped against an exposed nerve.

"Settle down, Sweden," Dharmander scolded. "We love a rowdy crowd, but not a mental crowd, all right?"

I caught Neil's eye as he passed behind me and gave him a sympathetic look. "It's like fookin' babysitting," he muttered irritably, his brogue seeming more pronounced than ever.

On stage, Dharmander let out a stilted laugh and squinted upwards at the overhead lights. "Where was I? Well, anyway, let's go through the rules. We are in Germany after all, so we have to have rules. Rule Number One is...and I'm talking to my Swedish crew at the moment... pleasepleasepleasepleaseplease don't talk during the sets. If a new comedian is on stage and you're talking, it can really fuck up their flow. So Rule Number One is one that I will really enforce, Okay? Because we want a friendly evening, don't we, Sweden?"

I braced myself for another manic howl, but relaxed as Dharmander's request engendered only vigorous-but-agreeable head bobbing from the third row. Most of the third row, anyway. One of the Swedes, a pale young man with wire-rimmed glasses and a thick, almost obscenely sensual mouth, appeared to have grown bored with the whole thing. He twisted his head to his right and began talking at the woman sitting next to him.

Dharmander made it through Rule Number Two without incident. If he noticed or was irritated by the bespectacled Swede's constant palaver, he didn't let it show.

"Rule Number Three," he informed us, "is please silence your cell phones. Or, actually, just put 'em on silent. We are in Berlin, the Party Capital of the World, which means at least eighty percent of you are waiting for a call from your drug dealer."

The mention of drugs penetrated the talking guy's unceasing chatter at the woman next to him. He dropped his head backward and emitted a series of excited yelps. "Gawlp! Gawlp! Gaaaaaaawlp!"

Dharmander's eyes flicked toward him. He looked down at the guy with a puzzled frown. "What's happening here?" he asked. Without waiting for an answer, he pivoted his head in the direction of one of the guy's co-workers. "Is he mental or something?"

The rest of the Swedes cheered. The co-worker nodded an eager affirmation.

"You there!" Dharmander said, returning his attention to the guy in the glasses. "Hey, buddy!"

The guy tilted his head upward, gazing at Dharmander with a look that seemed to ask, *What's the problem, bro?*

"Yes, you," Dharmander pressed. "What's your name, mate?"

The guy stared at him, saying nothing.

"His name is Erik," the woman next to him piped up.

"I thought that was Erik," Dharmander challenged, gesturing toward one of the other Swedes who was sitting a few seats over.

"He's Eric with a 'K' and that's Erik with a 'C'," she clarified in a light, chirping, voice.

"Ah, so that's nice Eric, and that's douchey Erik?" Dharmander pronounced, and this was received with a gleeful cheer of assent by the Swedes. It was the first time I had ever heard Dharmander overtly heckle an audience member, and I silently cheered him on, willing him to shut Erik-With-A-K down once and for all. The guy was seriously pissing me off. He was disrespecting the space and preventing me from getting my nightly fix of communitas.

Dharmander hovered over Erik-With-A-K, speaking to him as one would speak to a child. "It's not nice to be fucked with, is it?"

"No," Erik-With-A-K mumbled.

"No, it isn't!" Dharmander agreed. "So no more talking, 'cause we want to keep the vibe happy. Okay?"

Now directing his attention to the group of Swedes as a whole, he said, "Honestly, mates, I'm not fucking about. We love having a big group of you guys, but there are a lot of other people who also paid to come see the show. If you're being dicks, first we will slag you off and then we will kick you the fuck out. This isn't the Erik Show or the Olaf Show. We want you to have fun, but don't be a bunch of raucous twats, Okay?"

Now looking at the rest of us with a beseeching expression, "How about a round of applause for me telling them off?" he requested of us, and we did as we were asked. Even a few of the Swedes joined in.

I pounded my palms together and whistled. "Yeah!" I hollered.

At our response, Dharmander appeared to relax. "Before I bring on the first comedian, what I'll do is...since a lot of you guys aren't from here...I'll give you some tips about Berlin."

He pointed to Eric-With-A-C (aka "Nice Eric").

"Hey, Nice Eric, how many days are you guys here in Berlin?"

"We...uh...leave...uh...tomorrow," Eric-With-A-C responded, looking nervous at being singled out.

"And how long have you been here?"

"Six days."

"Six days!" Dharmander marveled, the light-hearted good cheer having returned to his voice. "This is why I love Swedish people! I didn't want to bring you guys into it now that you've finally settled down, but stand up and show everyone how fresh you look."

Eric-With-A-C stood up and turned to face the rest of us, indeed looking neat, guileless, and not long out of the womb. Under the pressure of our gaze, he began compulsively stuffing his hands into his pockets and taking them out. In, then out again.

"Amazing right?" Dharmander said. "After six days in Berlin, an English person is like..." He staggered backward on the stage with half-closed eyes, crumpling sideways onto the stool next to him. "'Aaaaaooooooooh!'" he mock-moaned, "I can't take anymore MDMA!'"

Hooting and laughter.

Dharmander stood up straight again. "But you Swedes have wonderful genes."

As he waited for our clapping to subside, Dharmander's dark brown eyes skimmed the pit, assessing the current conditions in front of him. In that brief gesture, I could see past his usual comic persona to a part of his personality that typically remained hidden over the course of a given show night. He always made hosting look easy, effortless. But now I could see that while he prowled around the stage playing the role of the (Un)Holy Fool, another part of him was always "minding the store"—reading the room, taking the temperature of our energies, making adjustments as needed to keep the evening flowing in a certain direction.

As our clapping dwindled, Dharmander nodded, as if satisfied. "Okay," he told us. "I think I've calmed shit down a bit. Are you guys ready for your first comedian?"

"YEAH!" we called out. I, for one, was more than ready for the show to begin. I was tired and looking forward to getting to bed.

Dharmander fished a small notecard out of the back pocket of his jeans and squinted at the name written on it. "Our first comedian's name is Emelia," he announced. "She comes to us all the way from Spain..."

A sudden movement in the third row caught his attention. Erik-With-A-K had started talking again, his thick mouth once again opening and closing, opening and closing, like a guppy in a fish tank gulping up briny food pellets. Seeing this, my teeth clamped together, a bubble of rage starting to build in my solar plexus.

"Erik!" Dharmander called out, sounding both pissed off and incredulous. "Buddy! I can see you talking. This is not Imax or Netflix, yeah? These are actual people up here on this stage."

He held one arm outward, palm facing upward in an imploring gesture. "Seriously, mate, shut the fuck up. If you don't, we are going to kick you the fuck out, and you're going to have to wait on the cold *Straße* all by yourself while all your friends are in here having fun. Okay?"

No response.

"Okay?"

Erik-With-A-K nodded slowly. Dharmander shook his head and pressed on. "Okay, then," he said. "Your first comedian's name is Emelia and she is from Spain. This is her first time here at Cosmic Comedy, so let's... Mate! Seriously!"

Erik-With-A-K had resumed talking. By now, all pretense of joviality had left Dharmander's face. His eyes burned dark neon, as if at any moment bright red lasers might come shooting out of each one like Cosmic Kitty on the club's logo.

Yes! I thought savagely. *Do it! Melt the fucker. End him.* Which was immediately followed by a second thought. *Holy shit, Hillary. Chill the fuck out.*

"Guys, help me out here," Dharmander said to the rest of us. "Anyone who wants Erik to shut the fuck up, on the count of three, shout 'Shut the fuck up!' Okay? Onetwothree!"

The sentiment was unanimous.

"SHUT THE FUCK UP!!!" we thundered, our many individual voices coming together as one exclamatory force. Some of the audience members raised their arms and pounded their fists into the air. Others cupped their hands around their mouths, creating fleshy megaphones to amplify their call. A grey-haired man in the corner stood partway up in an awkward crouch-squat, as if by doing so he could volley his words much more intensely at his target. As for me, I yelled the words at full volume, momentarily surprised at the wild, almost feral sound coming out of my throat. That surprise lasted only a nanosecond before being engulfed a red haze of fury in which no ambiguity could live. In my imagination, I was nothing more or less than a creature of Absolute Rightness. I had lost all desire to be polite and civilized, left only with an aching need to destroy the destroyer. The destroyer of what? The destroyer of our collective joy. I had a sudden image of us all running at Erik-With-A-K, tearing him apart. And while a distant part of me felt shame for such a violent, unenlightened, and, certainly, overblown urge, another part basked in the delicious, orgasmic release of tension resulting from the feeling of being on the inside of the mob with the sum total of our collective will projected at the unruly Swede who, for me at least, had become a psychological stand-in for every mad citizen or dictator who had ever aimed to gain control over existence. We in the audience had little power over the larger world, but within the microcosm of Cosmic Comedy's dark basement, we could have our say.

Dharmander moved quickly to the edge of the stage, staring down at Erik-With-A-K. "I'm not fucking with you, mate," he told him. "This is your last chance. If you don't shut the fuck up we're going to ask you to leave, right?"

Erik-With-A-K gaped at him with the bewildered air of one who is unsure where he is and how he got there.

"Hey!" Dharmander said, speaking the next four words with measured emphasis. "Do...you...understand...me?"

Erik-With-A-K nodded slowly.

"Okay," Dharmander said, straightening up. His shoulders dropped away from his ears as he returned to center stage. He smiled wanly at the rest of us and shrugged.

"Some people can't handle 18 percent shots," he said, almost apologetically.

There was scattered clapping around the audience. I put my forearms on the railing in front of me and slumped forward, feeling spent, although the evening had barely begun.

***

After that, the evening continued on more or less like any other. The Swedes slipped into a state of placid enthusiasm. The few times Erik-With-A-K's attention drifted briefly back to the woman next to him, Dharmander ignored him.

Only one of the comedians on the evening's lineup made mention of the earlier excitement.

"It's cool being in Berlin with such an international crowd," Jim Williams, an American expat living in Wroclaw, Poland, said. "I'm an American, in Germany, doing comedy in English, for a bunch of drunk Swedish people."

The Swedes let out a brief cheer at this.

"I'm so happy to be here," he continued. "It's crazy living in Poland. People always ask me...well, they used to ask me...'Why do you live in Poland?' And now it's like, 'Oooh, welcome American refugee. Please come on in.'"

***

At the end of the night, after the final comedian left the stage, Dharmander grabbed the microphone once again.

"Okay guys, that's the end of the comedy for tonight."

"Boo!" called out one of the Swedes.

Dharmander smiled at this, but it was a tired, obligatory smile, as if the evening had drained some of his life force.

"Aw, you guys are so nice now," he said. "Don't worry, we're here every single Monday and Thursday with our open mic shows and every single Friday and Saturday with our showcase. So please come back and visit us."

Speaking directly to Erik-With-A-K, "Yeah, mate, you can come back; you was nice in the end." And, then, almost to himself, "After the whole crowd told you to shut the fuck up, that is."

From there, Dharmander moved quickly and easily through his usual end-of-the-show ritual.

"...and apart from that," he said, hooking the thumb of his free hand into the front pocket of his jeans, "I really do want to thank you guys for coming out."

He offered us a tired smile. "The show started out a bit shaky, didn't it?"

Across the audience, heads bobbed in agreement.

"Yeah, it did. But that's all right. Because what Cosmic Comedy proves is that, even when we have a crazy show like tonight, we can manage that shit all by ourselves, yeah?"

"YEAH!" everyone around me shouted. A few minutes later, we were all heading up the stairs, out of the basement, and into the night. As for me, while the experience of collective joy left my cells buzzing with seeming unlimited energy and vitality, I was now feeling drained and queasy. By the time I reached my hotel, I was overcome with a crushing loneliness.

Chapter 12

Fight or Be Funny:
The Bitterness of Togetherness

The next afternoon, I met up with Marianne at the Russian café. It had become "our" spot. I told her everything that had gone down during the previous evening.

When I was done talking, she said, in a matter-of-fact tone of voice,

"There's some interesting work that has been done on the negative aspects of crowd psychosis," she said. "You should read Elias Canetti's *Crowds and Power*, which addresses the hypnotic nature of Nazi rallies."

I flinched at the comparison, followed by the clench of rising defensiveness. A rush of blood flew to my face. If Marianne noticed, she didn't say.

"Of course," she continued, "a comedy club is not the same as a mass of screaming fascists, but, in the end, crowds are crowds, aren't they? They all generate their own brand of mad logic."

I recoiled at her blunt assessment of the evening, thinking about the part I had played in it. She wasn't entirely wrong. In the sober light of day, I could recognize that my venomous reaction to the Swedes' disruption was overblown. And, yet...

"The guy was being a major pain in the ass," I insisted, trying to keep my voice casual. "He totally disrupted the evening."

She offered me a sympathetic eye roll.

"Trust me," she said, "if I had been there I would have been livid with him. Livid! But, you know, a comedy club is not a church. And the guy was just talking, not taking a piss on the cross or knifing people."

"Uh-huh," I said, stiffly, raising the coffee cup to my lips.

"Also," Marianne continued, her eyes flickering hesitantly toward me, "I wasn't going to say anything, but since we're talking along these lines, I feel I should tell you that while I definitely had fun at the club the other night I didn't find it quite as...transcendent as you do."

Her words hung in the air. On the other side of the restaurant, an elderly woman in a fur coat called out, "Ich möchte jetzt bestellen!" and the waitress dashed over to take her order.

"In fact," Marianne continued, "some of the sets made me pretty uncomfortable."

My hand twitched slightly, causing a splash of coffee to drop into the saucer. "Which ones?" I asked, still trying to sound cool and unaffected.

"Well, for one, the guy who imitated his girlfriend masturbating," Marianne said, screwing up her face in disgust at the memory. "I thought that was tasteless and rude. And also the guy who did the bit about drunk women approaching him at techno clubs and telling him how delicious he looks. I get that he was trying to make a larger point about the fetishization of Black bodies, but I thought it was extremely misogynistic."

"I know that guy," I said, feeling a heat rise within me. "He's not misogynistic at all."

Marianne shrugged. "Well, Okay, but what I'm trying to say is that while I respect Dharmander and Neil for what they're trying to do, for me, at least, it was most definitely not the 'Friendliest Place in the Universe.'"

***

In her book, *Communitas: The Anthropology of Collective Joy*, Edith Turner wrote, "When things are right, our friendship covers all of us like a tent." [1] But when things are not right—when the sense of communitas breaks down—there is the feeling of sliding apart from one another, along with a painful shattering of the beautiful illusion of a shared reality.

Years earlier, I had met two women. They were best friends, both synesthetes. For people with synesthesia, areas of the brain ordinarily separated and unrelated interact with one another, causing unusual cross-sensory communications. For example, a synesthete might "see" music or "hear" colors. These two women shared a form in which letters and numbers were associated with corresponding colors.

"Do you both see the same colors for the same letters?" I wanted to know. I was fascinated. Perhaps *they* were the ones perceiving reality

---

[1] Turner, E. (2012). *Communitas: The anthropology of collective joy*. New York: Palgrave Macmillan, xi.

correctly, more fully as *das Ding an sich*, the thing-in-itself. I had to know.

"Sometimes," one of the women said. "For example, many synesthetes see the letter 'O' as white."

The other woman nodded her head vigorously.

"Yes, it's white," she agreed.

"But," the first woman continued, "I see the letter 'R' as dark green..."

"When it's actually mauve," the other woman corrected.

The first woman stiffened. Frowned. She turned toward her friend slowly. "'R' is *green*," she repeated, her eyes narrowing.

At this, an eerie transformation took place between them. The two women assumed primal postures of aggression: shoulders drawn back; chests out; hands clenching and unclenching, stiff at their sides, not loose and gesturing as they had been. I could see the conflict arising not just *between* them, but *within* each of them as well. While, on the one hand, each recognized she was intellectually compelled to question the validity of her perception due to her diagnostic category as a synesthete, on another level each was ready to defend her perception of reality against anyone who threatened its veracity. The look on their faces was that of betrayal. Seconds later, they laughed at this impasse, and yet each one left the conversation with a dazed, unhappy look.

***

"Oh," I said in response to Marianne's sudden admission. And while the mature part of me had no problem understanding that two people may have different experiences of something, another aspect of my psyche responded to her words like a wounded animal—with extended claws and gnashing teeth, coming up with as many equations as I could to rationalize why her experience was based in projection and self-absorption, while my perception was pure and true.

This part of me thought: *She's a lesbian and therefore overly sensitive to certain issues. She's a South African and therefore probably unconsciously racist. She's stressed out about the environmental situation back home and therefore not able to appreciate what takes place there. She grew up religious and Dharmander's imitation of Jesus on the cross probably hit a nerve...*

Who was it who said the day inevitably comes for each one of us when we discover right down to the tips of our toes that we are an asshole?

Marianne regarded me with trepidation. "I'm sorry if I insulted your friend," she said.

"No problemmoooo," I drawled, clearly meaning the opposite.

"Are we good?" she asked and when I looked up and saw the sincerity in her eyes, the tightness in my chest softened.

"Yeah," I said. "Of course we are."

And I meant it, even though my heart was still beating fast. A bit later, Marianne and I said goodbye stiffly. The chasm between us was closing, but not yet fully sealed.

Back in my hotel room, I cranked open the window, letting the mercifully cold late-afternoon January air blow against my face. Outside, daylight was fading and the street lamps were popping on one by one. A cawing burst of laughter, followed by a gleeful shouting, rose up from the sidewalk as a pair of women exited the bakery below. The women interlinked arms and walked down the street together, each holding an overstuffed white paper bag in their free hands. Watching this, I felt fuzzy and unreal, as if I were a ghost haunting the third floor of the hotel while the physical world flowed below me in an endless river of cause and effect. While I had once sought out separateness—even craved the ability to float above it all in order to see everything complete—this feeling of total disengagement was nothing I had ever desired.

Why had I responded so savagely to Marianne's differing experience? After all, over the course of my time in Berlin, there had been sets at Cosmic Comedy that had crossed my own personal line of decency, kindness, and taste. One night, an Australian comic informed us that because of all the recent acts of terrorism his parents were nervous about him traveling so much. Across the audience, many heads nodded. To this, we could all relate. Over the course of the previous two years, several hundred people across seven different countries had been killed or injured when terrorists drove vans into large crowds. Death was everywhere.

But lately, the comedian continued, the terrorists didn't seem to be making the same effort that they used to. While the events of 9/11 had necessitated skill and planning, it seemed that lately all a terrorist mastermind needed was a bunch of really bad drivers.

At this, my stomach lurched, then dropped. Some jokes served to relieve the anxieties of traumatic events, while others danced on the grave of a broken world. For me, this set represented the latter. It offended my ears and mind and heart.

"No!" I interjected in a whooshing ejaculation, and in a seat near me, a woman moaned, "Too soon! *Toooo soooon.*"

On another evening, a comedian from Mumbai[2] did a set based on the conceit that all transgender women wanted to have "big tits and juicy lips. No one wants to be just like, an engineer," he mock-grumbled and then let out a nervous, high-pitched giggle. Around me, the audience emitted a collective groan. It was not a happy sound.

A hurt look crossed the comedian's face. "Jesus, I'm just telling jokes here," he whined.

The rest of his set was more or less the same. It was messy and offensive. It was all tension and no release. It didn't take us anywhere we wanted to go. When the comedian's time was up, those in the audience who applauded him did so lethargically.

Dharmander retrieved the microphone from him. "Ajay Talwar, ladies and gentlemen!" he said in a strained voice. "Doing his part to break the stereotype that Indians are sexist."

He laughed, but the laugh was nervous, stilted. When he spoke next, his voice had an apologetic sound. "Yep," he repeated, "breaking that stereotype."

It was one of the few times that I had heard Dharmander come close to publicly calling out a comedian's behavior, and I was glad of it, determined that such offenses should not stand. After the show, I asked Dharmander about it.

"Usually I try to say something positive after every comedian," he told me, "but in that case if I had done so I would have lost the confidence of the audience. I talked to him later and said, 'Mate, what were you trying to say there? What's your message? Because that was really offensive.'"

So, yes, there had been those moments for me as well, but I had considered them outliers, exceptions that proved the rule. I had pushed them out of my mind, not wanting to dwell there, only wanting to focus on the good, the funny, the joyful. Marianne had said that a comedy club wasn't a church, but the truth was that Cosmic Comedy had, for me, become a sacred space. Bound by the divine force of collective joy, liberated through our laughter, I had begun to believe that we *could* see from the perspective of Wim Wenders's angels, ecstatically aware of our fragile and frightened but nevertheless endearing humanity. Our own and that of those around us. It was a beautiful idea. The kind of beautiful idea I had always sought out.

---

[2] Name and personal details changed.

If you aren't afraid of where you came from, why are you afraid of where you are going?

But the painful reality was that every beautiful idea also holds the seeds of its opposite. For all collective joy's empathy-inducing powers, it also could be responsible for the madness of the crowd, for provoking a state of "solidarity" in which, as Edith Turner described it, "one group depends on the opposition of the alien group for its strength of feeling."[3] In the post-World War II memoir *A Woman in Berlin*, the eponymous author described the ways in which during the dark days of East Berlin's Russian occupation immediately following the war ordinary citizens turned upon one another. Reflecting on the vilification of one of her neighbors, she confessed, "I also gave him a piece of my mind, which bothers me right now. Does that mean that I, too, am following the mob? 'Hosanna! Crucify him!'—the eternal refrain."

Indeed. The eternal refrain. One to which we always seemed to return. And as the Night of the Unruly Swedes and my reaction to Marianne's judgments had proven, for all my progressive self-righteousness, I was no different. That opposing force was within me as well. The madness of the crowd was part of the predictable universe in which I participated and would likely always participate.

Struck by a sudden emotional vertigo, I pushed myself away from the window and collapsed backward onto the hotel bed. There would be a Cosmic Comedy show that night, but all I wanted to do was sleep and sleep and sleep for the next four days, until it was time to fly home. I would be leaving Berlin with my tail tucked between my legs and nothing to show for my work, but so what? It was time for me to let go of my naïve romanticism once and for all. All that was left for me to do was to emotionally retreat into a state of mind that went beyond even cynicism. I had to adopt a mental posture in which the painful discrepancy between the world as it was and the world as I wanted it to be could not penetrate my fragile psyche. There, I would await wherever the merciless spiral of history brought us, in uncaring numbness.

***

In the end, however, I decided to head over to Cosmic Comedy after all. I discovered I didn't want to be alone, drowning in my own dark thoughts.

---

[3] Turner, E. (2012). *Communitas: The anthropology of collective joy*. New York: Palgrave Macmillan, 5.

On stage, Dharmander flashed us his brightest of smiles. "You guys are such a great audience," he told us. "So I won't muck about. Our next comedian is the co-promoter of this show, as well as one of my best friends! He's my bruddah from another muddah! And you're going to fucking love him. Give it up for Neil Numb!"

This surprised me. I had thought that Neil was like me—the introvert always circling the perimeter. I let out an exhale. Apparently all my expectations and assumptions were destined to be crushed. That would have to be okay. It was time to get real.

Neil leaned casually on the speaker at stage left, microphone in one hand and a bottle of beer in the other. "Hello everyone. My name is Neil Numb and I am from Scotland...like so many other Scottish people."

A low but constant murmuring coming from the back of the audience caught his attention and he squinted toward the sound. "Are you translating back there in the dark, man?" Neil asked incredulously. "If so, it's going to be a long set for you."

Laughter across the audience. Neil returned his gaze to the rest of us.

"Anyway," he said, "if you don't already know, Scotland is basically the Dark Ages. You cannot buy alcohol after 10 pm. My very first night in Berlin, my friend and I get to Warschauer Straße Bridge and my friend's like, 'Fancy a beer?' And I'm like, 'Sounds cool. Which bar?' But he just pulls over, buys one on the side of the road, and hands me it. And I was like..."

Neil's arm, holding the microphone, dropped limply to his side. He stared straight ahead, looking at his imagined friend with wide-eyed wonder. As if about to weep with joy, he raised the microphone slowly to his mouth once more.

"I'm *home*."

Laughter and clapping. Neil broke into a warm grin and cackled along with us. "And that's how it happens, man. You come to Berlin for three weeks and then suddenly it's ten years later and you're like, 'Maybe I should sign up for some German courses.'"

He grabbed his beer off the speaker and took another swig as we hooted enthusiastically. "But, listen," he told us after he had placed the bottle back on the speaker, "I've gone *three days* without smoking."

At the sound of our applause, Neil's face grew stormy. He shook his head back and forth furiously.

"Don't fucking clap!" he cried. "I'm an embarrassment to Scotland! Yesterday I told my girlfriend, 'I've given up smoking!' And she's like, 'That's great. You also drink too much and should go to the gym.'

"She's trying to gentrify me, man!" Neil said, now looking like a man who was trying to make a quick escape out of an oil-slicked drum. "What's next? Death by natural causes? Absolutely not! I want to die like a fucking Scottish person!" Raising a fist out in front of him to shoulder height in a "victory" gesture, he growled, "By misadventure! I want to go like my granny. My grandmother, my mum's mum, was a fucking legend! She smoked sixty cigarettes a day her whole fucking life, like a true Scotswoman. And a least a bottle of whisky a day since she was like...I dunno...nine or something.

"When my granny was 85 years old, she went to the doctor and the doctor was like, 'Whatever you do, don't give up smoking, because it will probably kill you.' And it did kill her in the end—at ninety-fucking-eight years old! She knew she was dying, and her last words on this planet were: 'If...you...think...that...I'm...dying...without...a...glass...of...whiskey...and...a...cigarette...in...my...hand...you've...got...another...thing...coming!' So we pushed her to the window, she had a glass of whiskey, smoked a fucking cigarette, and then..."

Neil slumped his head down against his chest and let out a frog-like groan. Then he picked his head up again.

"My granny, ladies and gentlemen! A fucking legend!" He grabbed his beer off the speaker and took another swig as we pounded our palms in applause.

***

"Great set," I told Neil at the end of the night. "I didn't know you performed."

"Yah, I do," he nodded, and then chuckled. "Growing up in Scotland, you either had to fight or be funny. If you weren't a fighter then your only solution was to be funny, or you'd spend your life getting beaten up."

"So you chose to be funny?"

He gave me a half surprised, half indignant look.

"No! I was a fighter."

We both laughed.

"But, you know," he said, "that's how life is. Sometimes you go down one path and then you flip it back."

There was a loud rattle behind us as a half dozen beer bottles came tumbling down, rolling like candlepins across the flat plane of the wooden bar. The bartender scrambled to scoop them up. Neil dashed over to help. I took this opportunity to sneak away, out of the club and into the cold night.

Chapter 13

Flipping It Back: Navigating the Gap between the Real and the Ideal

Midway through *Wings of Desire*, the angel Damiel becomes enamored of a mortal woman, a beautiful but lonely circus performer. What was it about her that captured his attention above all other humans? Perhaps it was because, as a trapeze artist, she was unafraid of gravity, and thus represented the best of both human and angelic realms; literally the highs and the lows and everything in between.

The trapezist learns that her beloved circus—the place where she has found the acceptance that she craves—is bankrupt and must close.

"That's it," she thinks as she walks back to her trailer. "It's over. Not even a season. It begins, it always ends. Too good to be true.... Don't cry! That's how it is, shit happens. It's not always as you'd like."

Contemplating her future in the city, she thinks, "Berlin! Here I'm a foreigner, yet it's all so familiar. Anyway, I can't get lost. You always end up at the Wall."[1]

I could relate. Despite my best efforts to become perfectly righteous and perceptually free, I always eventually banged up against the wall of my own limited perception. Not to mention my insistence that the world should be one thing when it really was another. No, it wasn't always as you liked.

***

A few days later, I returned to the United States with my audio recorder full of the interviews I had conducted with Dharmander, Neil, and about half a dozen other comedians. Along with this, a notebook filled with scribbled personal reflections. Thanks to Dharmander and Neil's generosity, I also had access to hours and hours of video recordings of

---

[1] Wenders, W. (Director). (1987). *Wings of Desire* [Film]. Road Movies Filmproduktion [Production Company], Argos Films [Production Company], Westdeutscher Rundfunk (WDR) [Production Company], Wim Wenders Stiftung [Production Company].

every Cosmic Comedy show I had attended while I was in Berlin. My intent upon returning home had been to reread, re-watch, and re-listen to all of it, from there undergoing the process of identifying various themes that gave some sort of insight into the ways in which communitas arose at Cosmic Comedy.

But for the first couple weeks after arriving home, I let all my materials gather dust. My heart wasn't in it. It all felt too raw. When I told my husband everything that had happened while I was in Berlin, including my conversation with Marianne, he smiled and said,

"Personally, I'm thrilled you found someone who's not buying your premise. Now you can get to the good stuff—Life, with all its ambiguity and muck."

"Shit," I told him.

"Exactly," he said.

I knew he was right, just as Neil had been right when he said that sometimes you go down one path and then discover you have to "flip it back." In order to truly understand communitas as it appeared at Cosmic Comedy, I couldn't just look at one side of it. I had to come to terms with its destructive as well as its constructive aspects.

But how? I first returned to Edith Turner's book, hoping to find a clue as to how to proceed. But there was nothing. Apparently Edith Turner had been like me, unwilling or unable to look at the shadow side of collective joy, instead reflecting solely upon the good and positive feelings that arise from it.

She even admitted as much in her final chapter. "This book is obviously incomplete," she wrote. "...[for example] I have not dealt with the negative aspects of communitas, nor do I show tough realism: for instance, there are no statistics about how much good or harm communitas may do to people."[2]

And, so, I was left to wander through the ambiguity and muck alone. I sat down at my desk, queued up the first interview, and pressed play.

***

Neil's disembodied voice growled out of the speakers. I had just asked him a question about the general "friendliness" of the Berlin comedy scene.

---

[2] Turner, E. (2012). *Communitas: The anthropology of collective joy.* New York: Palgrave Macmillan, p. 222.

"For the most part the scene is great," he said. "But this is show business and like anywhere in show business, people are driven by their own self-interests. If you think most comedians wouldn't sell their own grandmothers for a Netflix special, then you're kidding yourself. That's just the way it is, and if you were expecting it to be any other way then maybe you're a little bit naïve."

I winced slightly at Neil's words, which now hit home in a way that they hadn't during the original conversation. But then the effusive energy of Dharmander's voice on the recording pulled me back to the moment.

"What will really fuck me off badly is when I feel like we're being taken advantage of," Dharmander said. "Or when people are openly going around slagging us off or purposefully trying to destroy what we've created by saying lies."

"Like what?" I heard myself ask, to which Dharmander responded, "Like saying that the reason that Cosmic is so popular is that we strong-arm people into the club or that we let people in for free or because we're giving away free pizza and shots. There are times when I think, 'Fuck this, man. This isn't worth my energy and it's not worth my fucking *chi*. You know what, guys? You win. If you guys think the scene is better without Cosmic, then fuck Cosmic and fuck you guys.' But then my common sense kicks in and I'm like, 'No, I'm not going to let those cunts win in that way.'"

"Dhar is much more sensitive than I am," Neil piped up, and, at this, Dharmander let out a good-natured laugh.

"Yeah," he said, "I am a sensitive little bitch. I go from…"

A moment of silence on the recording as Dharmander offered us a sweet, beaming smile.

"To what?" I asked.

"To 'I really want to fuck that guy up!'" he growled.

"Then you see the dark side of Dharmander," Neil said.

"What does that look like?"

"That's pretty much it," Neil replied. "He still has a big smile."

"But it doesn't bother you as much?" I asked Neil.

"Eh, I don't care."

"Oh come on man," Dharmander countered. "There have been times…"

"It used to really bother me a lot," Neil agreed, "but now I'm just like…puh. It's a lot of energy wasted."

"Yeah, yeah," Dharmander drawled, and then, "He's good now but it used to be that I'd wake up in the morning and see that at 4:30 a.m. Neil had posted, 'You all can go fuck yourselves!'"

"That's true," Neil admitted.

He laughed, and Dharmander and I joined him.

***

Later, toward the end of the same conversation, Neil said, "You should talk to Caroline Clifford. She's the godmother of the Berlin comedy scene and one of the early champions of the movement."

And so I did. In 2006, Caroline left a successful London stand-up career to come to Berlin. Not long afterwards, she, along with American comedian Paul Salamone, started one of the city's first weekly comedy shows, followed by the development of the Berlin Stand-Up School. Over the next several years, the Berlin stand-up community grew exponentially, becoming (according to some, anyway) the largest English-speaking comedy scene in a foreign-language country.

When I mentioned to Caroline that Neil had referred to her as the "Godmother of Berlin Comedy," she shrugged and said, "I didn't set out to earn the name, but if I have in any way earned it, it's because it was very important to me to try to avoid some of the pitfalls that I saw in London. I wanted to move it in a way that people weren't just out for their own interests. I've always tried to get people to think more about the community as a whole. For example, 'Don't start up a new show just for your own interests, for your own profits. Think about this small community and whether what you're offering really needs to be here.' I know I won't get through to everybody, but I think on the whole that message has been positively received because that attitude has become a core part of the scene. We're not stepping on each other's toes. It's relatively respectful."

By the time I arrived in January 2018, Caroline's other website, ComedyInEnglish.com, listed more than two-dozen stand-up events occurring throughout the city on a given week. There was a monthly show geared toward promoting the work of female comedians, LGBTQ comedians, and comedians from other under-represented groups. There was one devoted to the theme of vegetables and another in which each comedian would perform twice: first straight, then drunk or stoned. American expat Belina Raffy's ongoing class, "Sustainable Stand-Up," was designed to teach non-comedians how to make important ideas "human, engaging, and deeply funny" through the use of stand-up techniques. As Caroline had hoped, the Berlin comedy scene was, in so many ways, a finely tuned ecosystem, one that survived and thrived due to a remarkable symbiosis among its members.

But, as with any ecosystem—perfectly balanced or not—it wasn't all absolute harmony and joyful togetherness. Egos came into play. Relations of power superseded relations of alliance. Ambitions overshadowed community spirit. Friendships ended over betrayals and/or mismatched expectations. And, as Marianne had experienced, despite Dharmander and Neil's best efforts to make it so, not everyone found Cosmic Comedy to be a wholly "friendly" or supportive place.

One afternoon, I met up with English comedian Josie Parkinson, the originator of "Sauce," the aforementioned stand-up show geared toward promoting the work of comedians from under-represented groups. Thinking back on Caroline's credo that the comedians should look for a true "need" before creating a new show, I asked Josie about her motivation for starting Sauce.

Her pleasant, lilting voice floated up out of the audio recorder's tinny speaker. "The Berlin stand-up scene is still very new and quite white-male dominated," she explained. "One time I was guest hosting at Cosmic Comedy and there was a male comedian on the stage who was saying things like, 'Some women think I'm going to harass them, and I'm like, have you seen yourself?' Basically, a version of 'Do you really think you are hot enough to be raped?' That was a really difficult moment for me, not knowing where my responsibility lay. Was I supposed to go up on stage afterward and say something like, 'Well, *that* was a load of shit. Don't give it up for that guy.' Or should I just brush it off?"

"What did you do?" I heard myself ask.

"It was not a very triumphant moment for me," she replied. "I have sort of blanked it out. I didn't confront him, but I remember trying to find a link by going back to how he talked about hummus, and just was like 'Hummus! Yeah! Okay.' It actually left me so flustered that I froze on stage later on in the show before bringing on the final act. I wouldn't have dealt with it the same way now, with another year's experience under my belt. It's crazy, because obviously I had a lot of information in my possession before even starting to think about what it would be like to work with male comedians who did not care about the feelings of their female colleagues or audience members, so it was almost like I had been spoiling for that fight. But, when it finally came, I didn't know what to do or say to make it better."

And then, "That's a bit of a downer," she said. "I'm sorry."

"No," I told her. "It's not a downer. It's beautifully human and relatable. There have been so many times in my own life in which I've wished I'd been the 'warrior' in real life that I am in my imagination. But reality is more complex."

It was true. Reality *was* complex. Much more so than the anticipatory ideals that we work out in our minds. But this was a necessary, even a good thing. Hadn't I complained on more than one occasion—most recently while mourning the gentrification of my hometown—that something died inside of us whenever life become overly homogenized, when the world and its features got whittled down to a series of identical landscapes? Yes, indeed. The irony was that while I demanded complexity and unpredictability in certain areas of life, so much of my existence, both personal and professional, had been dedicated to seeking out a single organizing principle under which all the chaos and confusion might rest. A God substitute. Something solid and unchanging that would solve X across all times, places, peoples, and circumstances. I had desired it so much, in fact, that I had placed that same divine burden on the joyful togetherness I had experienced at Cosmic Comedy. So much so that when anyone presented contradictory information, I glossed over it, not wanting to blemish the beautiful, idealistic picture that I had been creating. When Marianne had admitted that her enthusiasm toward Cosmic Comedy had not matched my own—that, like Josie, what she had experienced there bordered on something closer to "anti-communitas"—all the hope I had placed in communitas as an all-encompassing solution to the ills of the world were thrown into a painful rupture.

When it comes to collective joy, one size does not fit all. Like most everything else, communitas is messy. One cannot homogenize it or pin it down. Communitas is a shapeshifter, showing up in different places and under different circumstances, taking the form most resonant to each individual's personal matrix of belonging.

"The shots are all the same," Dharmander would often say in his happy host's voice as audience members drifted down the stairs each evening. "They're just in different glasses, like we are as people!" And while I had always smiled when I heard him offer up this cheeky and life-positive refrain, what I had discovered was that at the same time I cheered on this sentiment—believing in the necessary diversity of us all—there also existed a fearful little fascist inside me who wanted to reduce the world to a single, shoutable slogan. In the absence of God and angels, the fate of our fragmented world appeared to depend upon the discovery of some sort of singularity to bind us all together. And when the experience of collective joy at Cosmic Comedy fell short of this impossible goal, the beautiful illusion of its possibilities was ripped away. What I was left with was the terror of raw confrontation with the world as it was.

Chapter 14

The Hunger for Perfection:
Facing the World As It Is

French-Cuban author Anaïs Nin wrote, "The more I explore neuroticism the more I become aware that it is a modern form of romanticism. It stems from the same source, a hunger for perfection, an obsession with living out what one has imagined, and if it is found to be illusory, a rejection of reality."[1]

When had I first rejected reality as it was? Was it on the day that my father's words about the non-existence of God and Heaven awoke in me a fever to seek out a new singularity, something to fill that empty space inside that would reconcile all the chaos of the world? As I considered this possibility, a new memory flooded forth, one that I had filed away in the back of my mind but now spilled over and demanded to be placed into the new equation that was forming.

***

In the spring of 2001, my father lay dying in a hospital bed. The way he looked during those last few days of his life...he looked like an apple left too long on the kitchen counter, its peel becoming wrinkled and sagged over the desiccated and shrunken fruit inside.

I sat with him. It was weirdly bright outside, like a reverse eclipse.

"Are you scared?" I asked him. Years ago, he had told me that if we weren't afraid of where we came from, we shouldn't be afraid of where we were going. I wanted to know if he still believed this, now that his time to go had come.

"I'm not scared," he told me. "I'm just sad."

And then he cried. And I cried, too—partially from grief, but also partly from the pain of witnessing another human being discover a harsh truth: that the force of their personal will was not enough. That

---

[1] Nin, A. (1969). *The diary of Anaïs Nin, 1934–1939*. New York: Mariner Books, 2.

the Universe had not made an exception for wonderful us. That it had not decided we were load-bearing features in the architecture of existence and would not spare us from the common problem of death.

I grieved our lack of specialness. His and mine.

Days later, when my father died, my stepmother called me. "Your father is with the angels now," she told me through her tears, and her words startled me, eclipsing even my grief. In that moment, all I could do was wonder if my stepmother was simply telling me what she thought I needed to hear or if my father had had a radical change of heart in the years since that day in the living room when he and I first talked theology and the finer points of cannibalism. Or—and this was what really caught my breath, hijacking all other thought—had his original proclamation about the absence of God and Heaven been, for him, a throwaway line, something said in haste but not fully believed, but which for me had become the foundation upon which I had built a life?

I couldn't ask him. I would never know. But as I sat at my desk staring at my audio recorder, I knew one thing for certain: I was tired of rejecting the world as it was. I was tired of seeking out utopias and then becoming cynical, even nihilistic, when the gap between the ideal and the real remained. I wanted to be more like Wim Wenders' angel, Damiel, who not only understood that human existence involved as much conflict as it did joyful togetherness, but actually reveled in the idea of all the Self–Other collisions of the finite world.

He decides to fall. To give up his angelic form and become a mortal human.

"I'm going to enter the river…" he tells Cassiel. "First, I'll have a bath. Then I'll be shaved by a Turkish barber who will massage me down to the fingertips…. If someone stumbles over my legs, he'll have to apologize. I'll be pushed around, and I'll push back…" He smiles. "This will be my first day."[2]

The first time I saw the film, I thought: *Is he crazy? Who would choose to be part of this human madness?*

Which was followed by a second, even more bitter, idea: *No wonder the skies are empty, with all these damned angels bailing on us.*

But that was then. Now, after my experience in Berlin, I realized that after a lifetime of longing for something pure and unadulterated—some

---

[2] Wenders, W. (Director). (1987). *Wings of desire* [Film]. Road Movies Filmproduktion [Production Company], Argos Films [Production Company], Westdeutscher Rundfunk (WDR) [Production Company], Wim Wenders Stiftung [Production Company].

sort of unfailing morning star to guide us to a better, more joyful way of being together—what I now needed was a new way of relating to the world, one that allowed me to navigate the emotional impact of living in a world in which both the light and dark sides of existence will always exist side by side. Rather than negating it, this was a key to understanding communitas.

Chapter 15

Stones in the Ocean:
The Communitas of Conflict

Due to its overcast winter months, Berlin had been dubbed "The Grey City." Indeed, during the entire three weeks of my trip that January, the sky had remained a mottled, piebald thing, hanging low in the atmosphere, its varied shades of grey temporarily compressing the world.

On stage at Cosmic Comedy, Jetset Ty Rone, the American comedian whom I had met early on in my trip, bemoaned the city's lack of wintertime sun.

"How y'all motherfuckers doing?" he asked us. "You doing good? Y'all motherfuckers loving Berlin?"

Clapping and cheering.

Jetset Ty Rone nodded. "Yeeeaaah...mmmm...I loooove this city. For real. I've been out here since August, man, and it's changed my life."

A young woman in the front row started clapping enthusiastically, and then, realizing she was alone in doing so, stopped abruptly and shoved her hands self-consciously into her armpits.

"Yeah, girl!" Jetset Ty Rone said to her. "Go ahead and clap, baby! You feel like clapping, you just clap whenever."

Scattered whoops across the audience at this.

"But, yeah," Jetset Ty Rone continued, "Berlin has changed my life! Before I moved here, I used to think about sex all the time. It was like a sexual addiction. Always going out, going to the clubs. Going on all those websites trying to meet girls, trying to find a woman and shit. But since I've moved to Berlin, I am completely cured. I don't think about women anymore. Now the only thing I fantasize about is sunlight."

A burst of unanimous laughter.

"Yeeeaaaaah," he said, slowly, sensually. "I want to put my fingers in some sunlight."

A melting smile spread across his face. He brought his fingertips up to his nose and inhaled deeply.

"It's like, 'Oh man, give me some sunlight!' It's been so long that now I think the problem is me. Like there's something that *I'm* doing that keeps sunlight away. Where am I going to find it? Where am I going to get it? I've got pictures of clear, sunny skies on my phone. I have dreams about it. I dreamt about the warm sun on my face. Turned out it was my roommate's cat. Get the fuck off me, man! Oh, but it was a beautiful dream…"

The woman in the front, now emboldened, shouted out: "It's so sad!"

"It *is* so sad," Jetset Ty Rone agreed. "There ain't no motherfucking sun! Where's the sun at? It's fucked up, you know what I mean?"

He shook his head. "Another thing about Berlin, and I never thought I'd say it, is that I be loving the police out here. For real! I'm from Los Angeles, right? I'm from America. And it is racist as hell out there. But Berlin police officers…they are cooler than any other cops! I'll be walking past them, like all scared and shit, and they don't even look at me. And then I'm just like…"

He looked at the back of his hand with a perplexed frown, "Am I still Black? It's crazy man, the other day I was coming from the train station and this dude ran past me and the police was running after him. And then when the guy hit the corner, he really put the jets on."

He mimed running really fast. "And the cops, one minute they were running…"

Here, he jogged in place, "And then, as soon as the guy hit the corner and took off, they were just like…"

He stopped running, wrinkled up his face in an exasperated frown and flapped one hand in the direction of the guys running, as if to say, *Forget this.*

"They started rolling cigarettes and shit! And I was like, goddaaaamn, this is amazing. If we were in LA, they would have the helicopters out."

His eyes were half closed, an expression of pure bliss."Beeeeeerlin," he purred in adoration, stretching the word to its fullest capacity.

One afternoon, Jetset Ty Rone and I met up at a curry restaurant in Neukölln. Dharmander and an Irish comedian and another comedian from Czechoslovakia joined us for lunch and then, once the meal was finished and the plates cleared, the three of them took off in various directions. While I fumbled with my audio recorder, Jetset Ty Rone excused himself, disappearing into the back of the restaurant. A few minutes later he reappeared, and sat down.

"I had to take a shit," he told me in a casual, conversational tone. "I feel better now."

"Excellent," I said, and listening to this again back at home weeks later, I couldn't help but grin all over again. That was one of the things that I loved about the comedians I had met: No part of one's humanity was off the table for revelation.

I asked Jetset Ty Rone my first question, but he didn't hear me. Instead, his eyes scanned the sidewalk outside. "It's so weird," he said, his voice on the recording becoming slightly dimmer as he pulled away from it, craning his neck to get a better look onto the street. "I keep seeing people that I know from the comedy scene. That guy with the glasses over there, walking away? His name is Ted…uh…Ted-something. He's always at comedy shows."

He turned his attention back to me.

"What did you ask me?"

"I asked if you ever miss the United States."

There was a brief pause, and then Jetset Ty Rone said, almost begrudgingly, "Yeah. Yeah, I do. I hate to say it, but despite all the fucked-up shit that goes on there, that *is* home."

He tapped his spoon on the table one, twice, then a third time. "But if I'd stayed in LA this whole time, I probably would have killed myself," he said. "It's such a horrible place to live, unless you've got money. It's not good for artistic endeavors. But since I came to Berlin and I started doing stand-up, it's like my confidence level, my self-awareness, who I am, certain things are all starting to fall into place. I'm learning more of what I like and what I don't like, shit that I stand for, shit that I don't stand for."

The waiter approached our table, asking us what else he might bring us.

"*Nein bitte, nein bitte*," Jetset Ty Rone said, and then after the waiter had gone, he continued. "You can *focus* here. That's the main thing. People say Germans are unfriendly, but…shit, no one's throwing bottles at me and calling me the N-word here. They leave me alone. I just want to be left alone to do shit and experience things. Because the shit you experience becomes the shit you do on stage."

Silence on the recording. The squeak of a chair. The clatter of dishes in the background.

"Right now I look at Berlin as a training ground," he told me. "Everything that happens here, whether I kill or whether I bomb, whatever good or bad happens, it's all a learning experience. Maybe I have a bad show, but instead of being sad and like, 'Oh that show was terrible,' I'll be like, 'Fuck, I'm glad that happened now and I experienced this now, so I know what to do next time.' Because in another situation—in LA or New York or London—if you get knocked down, it's going to take two or three years to crawl back. It's very unforgiving."

I had a memory of Jetset Ty Rone spreading his arms out wide at this point, as if to encompass the whole world.

"But in Berlin!" he exclaimed. "Man, you can be one of the shittiest comedians out there and Dharmander and Neil will give you a spot. It's crazy! The hottest comedy club in town and you can still get up and perform. Nowhere else in the world would you get that kind of opportunity."

There was a soft thud of heavy glass landing on wood as he placed the bottle of Club-Mate that he had been holding back down onto the table.

"Yeah, that's the beauty of Berlin," he said. "You can fall here. You can fall *hard* and get right back up and keep on trying. That's why I'm here. And that's why I'm going to stick around until shit changes."

"Do you think it will change?" I heard myself ask.

Jetset Ty Rone responded immediately. "Everything changes," he told me, and his voice held a hint of incredulity at my question. "Berlin is the best place right now, but once the word gets out, it will be packed with comics."

"I guess that's inevitable," I said, and I could hear a faint misery permeating my voice.

"Of course it's inevitable," he replied. "And it'll be both good and bad depending on how you look at it. But if you look at it the right way it will always be good. Right now, it's the same people over and over again. There's no fresh blood, no fresh meat. Shit gets stale. Same jokes. Same premises. Always another Nazi joke. More people coming out here will make it more interesting. It's going to force people to take it more seriously. Myself included. We'll be like a bunch of stones in the ocean rubbing up against each other, making each other smoother, more polished.

"And," Jetset Ty Rone said, as if this should have been self-evident, "once Berlin changes, there'll be a new Berlin someplace else. A new city where it's all happening. Maybe it'll be in the Czech Republic. Maybe Hungary. Maybe after Trump, the dollar will collapse and there will be a big social upheaval and Detroit will be the place to be where the shit is going down. There's always an artistic center somewhere. It was Paris once. It was New York in the '70s. Scorsese and all those greats came out of that. Hip hop came out of that. There was San Francisco in the '50s and the '60s with all the Beatnik shit."

Outside the restaurant, a delivery truck heaved and rumbled over the cobblestone street.

"But for right now, Berlin is still ours," he told me. "And those of us who are here now are making this shit what we want it to be."

***

Back at home, I rewound the recording in order to listen to this part again.

"More people coming out here will make it more interesting," Jetset Ty Rone's voice echoed through the speaker once again, "We'll be like a bunch of stones in the ocean rubbing up against each other, making each other smoother, more polished."

I leaned back in my chair and closed my eyes. It was a beautiful image, this idea that it was because of—and not despite—the friction of Self–Other interactions that we evolve into better, more polished versions of ourselves. And one that was not without philosophical precedence. In graduate school, I had become enamored of the philosophy of the 18th/19th-century German Idealist philosopher G.W.F. Hegel. In his "dialectic model," Hegel had put forward a theory that humanity's evolution toward greater forms of Being was dependent upon the confrontation of opposing energies, entities, and ideas. In its most stripped-down version (one free from the many economic and political ideologies that would eventually claim it as inspiration), Hegel's dialectic went something like this:

In the beginning, a *thesis*—a singular, undifferentiated entity, energy, or idea—arises. At first, it is completely alone, representing the totality of all existence. But this state of absolute aloneness is unsustainable. No life can come out of it, for all energies, entities, or ideas must interact with other energies, entities, or ideas in order to grow and reach their fullest capacities. (As one of my research participants in a previous project had once said to me, "You may know yourself, but you can never *see* yourself. For that you need another."[1]) Out of this lonely and stagnant state, an *antithesis*—an opposing energy, entity, or idea—arises and makes itself known. While the appearance of this new, opposing force fulfills the original thesis's yearning for a non-self "other" by which to come to know itself, it eventually becomes

---

[1] Webb, H.S. (2012). *Yanantin and masintin in the Andean world: Complementary dualism in modern Peru.* Albuquerque, NM: University of New Mexico Press, 139.

an existential threat to the original. Both desire to control the world, to shape it in its own image.

A power struggle ensues. The original thesis and emerging antithesis fight it out, exchanging energies until, eventually, out of this confrontation, a third entity—energy or idea—is created, a synthesis that both contains and transcends the original two. This Third Thing restores harmony for a while. But like the original thesis before it, the new entity, energy, or idea eventually becomes lonely and unfulfilled in its singular state. Just as before, in order to evolve beyond itself, it must invoke its opposite. The cycle of conflict and resolution begins all over again. Hegel believed that this dialectical pattern would occur over and over again until humanity achieved a final state of Absolute Knowledge.

Of course, Hegel was a teleological thinker like me, always placing himself on the outside of things, determined to get an unblemished grasp of the whole, always looking to find a means to some final, blissful end. Hegel's critics argued that the cold rationalism of the dialectic model was too far removed from the realities of daily living. As the philosopher Søren Kierkegaard put it, "Life can only be understood backwards; but it must be lived forwards."

Or, as the angel Damiel says as he and Cassiel stroll down the Death Strip just prior to Damiel renouncing his angelhood and taking human form, "To look is not to look from on high, but at eye level."[2]

***

His decision made, Damiel falls. There is no drama about it, no long, drawn-out metamorphosis from one thing to another, just the acknowledgment of a choice, and then an instantaneous rebirth into mortal form. As this occurs, the film turns from its previous lens of black and white into color, signifying that Damiel is now a full sensory participant in the finite world.

One of the first things Damiel experiences as a mortal man is the color and taste of the blood from the back of his head, which has split open as the result of his angelic armor falling on top of him. He touches the wound, then looks at his hand, perplexed.

Blood. Red.

[2] Wenders, W. (Director). (1987). *Wings of Desire* [Film]. Road Movies Filmproduktion [Production Company], Argos Films [Production Company], Westdeutscher Rundfunk (WDR) [Production Company], Wim Wenders Stiftung [Production Company].

He puts his fingers to his tongue. A smile of wonder spreads across his face.

"Now I begin to understand," he murmurs to himself.[3]

***

I was beginning to understand as well. Not everything, but enough. Something, at least, that I could live with happily. Despite my comfort at hovering above things hoping to see everything complete, in order to understand communitas as it appeared at Cosmic Comedy and on the Berlin stand-up scene, I needed to consider it from eye level. I needed to look at the ways in which it played out—and, indeed, could only be played out—through the dialectical tension and resolution of those engaging within it.

For example, having rubbed up against the "bear pit" nature of so much of the stand-up comedy world and finding it lacking in kindness, Dharmander and Neil had created its antithesis, a venue that was designed to be a most friendly place.

"We're comedians," Dharmander told me. "We're creating the kind of club that we want to perform in."

For so many, this made Cosmic Comedy an ideal spot to work their craft, to get stage time, and to gain confidence. But not everyone experienced it this way. Josie Parkinson had had a very different encounter, but rather than falling into despair and quitting the scene altogether, she had created Sauce. Not only did such a show fill a need for those who felt marginalized on the Berlin comedy scene, but just the simple fact of its existence initiated a ripple effect that engendered greater empathy and understanding within the community as a whole.

"Sauce has allowed people to become more aware of certain issues, and because of that there have been some changes in the scene," Josie said. "For example, one of my friends, Jetset Ty Rone, hosts another show in town. The last time he booked me for his show, he messaged me and the two other women in the lineup and told us, 'I'm thinking of putting these two guys on the same bill. If you have any problems with them, just say so and I'll take them off, no questions asked.' So people are thinking more about these things."

---

[3] Wenders, W. (Director). (1987). *Wings of Desire* [Film]. Road Movies Filmproduktion [Production Company], Argos Films [Production Company], Westdeutscher Rundfunk (WDR) [Production Company], Wim Wenders Stiftung [Production Company].

A happy outcome. But, of course, as Hegel pointed out, the synthesis that resolves the original conflict never remains unopposed for long.

"Then again," Josie added, somewhat sadly, "at the same time that this is happening, there are also comedians who are responding to this growth and advancement by doubling down on their outmoded views."

One thing inevitably calls to it its opposite, setting off a new series of conflicts. The joy and madness of the crowd arise in tandem, initiating a new revolution of the dialectic. Communitas—both its light and dark aspects—was like gravity. It made us fall together. Sometimes painfully so. This was the true journey of parallel beings. In this way, our lives—and the stories that came out of them—became intertwined, changing each of us in little and big ways.

***

Now a mortal man, Damiel wanders West Berlin, searching for the trapezist. That night, he goes to a rock-and-roll club. She is there. She sees him. She knows him. His presence has penetrated her dreams, just as the potential for connection and understanding and togetherness invades so many of our dreams. She approaches him. He hands her a glass of wine, then moves toward her. She places a hand on his chest, stopping him. He stops.

"I want to tell you about a girl," she tells him. "When I was with someone, I was often happy. But at the same time, it all seemed a coincidence. These people were my parents, but it could have been others. Why was this brown-eyed boy my brother and not the green-eyed boy on the opposite platform? The taxi driver's daughter was my friend, but I might as well have put my arm round a horse's neck..."

Damiel takes her hand, leans in toward her. After a bit, her face lights up, as if in a state of revelation.

"I must put an end to coincidence!" she says. "I don't know if there's destiny, but there's a decision. *Decide!*... [T]he whole world is taking part in our decision."[4]

***

---

[4] Wenders, W. (Director). (1987). *Wings of Desire* [Film]. Road Movies Filmproduktion [Production Company], Argos Films [Production Company], Westdeutscher Rundfunk (WDR) [Production Company], Wim Wenders Stiftung [Production Company].

Like Damiel, like the trapezist, in order to approach communitas on its own terms, I had to decide.

Decide what, exactly?

Decide to quit fighting reality. Decide to stop searching for some absolutely harmonious world that would never exist. Decide to let go of all these impulses toward perfection or nothing and simply show up. Show up and participate, despite the personal risks inherent within that choice.

But, then again, I suddenly realized, I'd been doing that all along.

"Berlin is awesome," the café owner's daughter had told me months earlier. "You should go."

And I had. And, as a result of that choice, new realities had been set in motion. Not just for me, but for others as well.

On my final day in Berlin before flying home, Marianne and I met at the Russian café one last time. Things were good between us again. The chasm had closed, our previous bond restored.

"So," Marianne sighed, after the waitress dropped off our drinks, "you leave tomorrow."

I nodded.

"Did you get what you needed from this trip?"

"Yes," I said. "And you were a big part of that."

She nodded, needing no explanation. There was a long pause between us, and then, "I'm terrible at goodbyes," she confessed, "but I do want to say that it's been genuinely lovely having you here. You have made this bleak Berlin winter infinitely more fun. Our connection comes at the right time for me. Watching you follow this thread of yours has been inspiring. It has opened up something for me as well, reminding me of my own relationship to Berlin and why I came here. It's exactly what I needed right now."

Later, we hugged goodbye, with promises to keep in touch. Marianne jumped on her bicycle and rode off in the direction of Volkspark.

Similarly, on one of my future research trips, Dharmander would tell me, "It's been really good for me to have you here, observing us. It's forced me to reflect on what we're trying to do at Cosmic Comedy and where we want to take it from here."

This pleased me.

Of course, not every ripple effect initiated by my presence in Berlin was perceived as positive. At least one comedian whom I later queried about using an excerpt of his set in this book declined, expressing discomfort that he had been under someone's analytical gaze in this way. Others ignored my requests. One became upset with my representation of Cosmic Comedy as "The Friendliest Place in the Universe."

For me, the temptation had always been to withdraw my participation from the world, not wanting anything I ever did to have any negative, unintended effects. But this feedback caused me to look at my assumptions and expand my understanding of the ways in which my experience diverged from that of others. As a result, I believe I came to a better understanding of communitas's various shapes, and the ways in which it ebbs and flows among us. It also prompted me to reevaluate my prior cynicism, silencing that voice that would sometimes ask: *Why bother trying to make a better world?* I now understood that my desire to build that better world wasn't an impulse begat out of childishness or boredom or privilege or naïve romanticism. Each of us was the dialectic in action, playing itself out over and over again. In the end, none of us could ever step outside of it. We could not become *das Ding an sich*, a totally separate thing unaffected by others. It was arrogance that made us think that we could do so. And a kind of madness that made us want to try. Through the joys and pains of our mutual engagement, together we birthed the world into being, over and over again. Perhaps that was why, as Edith Turner pointed out, communitas "create[s] more than history; it has its imprint on eternity."

Epilogue

A few hours after saying goodbye to Marianne, I made my way over to Cosmic Comedy for the final show of that first research trip. Upon arriving at the club, I sat down at the entrance with Dharmander and some of the comedians. Neil waved to me as he hurried onward toward some task. He was wearing the T-shirt I had given him when I first arrived—the one with the logo of the Turkish café from my hometown. It was far too big for him, but he wore it anyway. That meant something to me.

Henning, the comedian from Liepzig, sat down on the bench next to me. "Did you know that as of today the Berlin Wall has been down longer than it was up?" he said, and, with that, I flashed backward to that morning in high school when Mr. Betterly excitedly informed us that the Berlin Wall had been torn down. Mr. Betterly had passed away several years earlier, and I wished very much that I could tell him that now, finally, I understood his enthusiasm.

***

That night, a skinny, middle-aged man took the stage. "My name is Doug and I'm from New Zealand."[1]

Scattered clapping at this.

"Which part of New Zealand?" a guy sitting in the back called out.

The comedian's head snapped up, startled. "Huh?" he asked, looking around to identify where the voice came from.

"Which part of New Zealand?" the audience member repeated.

"Uh," the comedian stammered. "Jeez, I didn't know I was going to be fielding questions during this set. Does anyone else in the audience have any questions for me?"

Laughter. The comedian smirked and turned back to the man who had spoken. "Have you been to New Zealand, sir?"

"I'm from there, too," the man said.

"Okay, where?"

---

[1] Name and details changed.

"Tauranga."

"Cool, man," the comedian, replied crisply. "I'm from Wellington."

The audience member gave him a thumbs up.

"I'm happy you approve," the comedian responded, then hesitated. "Do you want to keep going with this convo, or shall I maybe do some jokes now?"

"Sorry," the man in the back said, looking chagrined.

"That's cool, man," the comedian said. "I'm glad you're enthusiastic. Uh...Where the fuck was I?"

At the end of the night, just before his closing speech in which he thanked us all for our participation, Dharmander led us all in singing Happy Birthday to one of the audience members. She had just turned 25.

When we were finished, he told her, "Because you decided to spend your birthday with us, we're going to give you a free Cosmic Comedy mug on your way out!"

From somewhere in the back came Neil's voice, calling out in a mock-horrified yell: "FREEEEEEEE???"

At this, we all erupted in laughter, proving that even in those dark days of time's spiral, not everything was falling apart or going in the wrong direction. Along with the pizza and apple schnapps, there at Cosmic Comedy we were digesting the world and all its current confrontations. No matter where on the planet we were from, all of us sitting in that dark basement were in the same unsettling position of not knowing what was going to happen next. Indeed, the next few years would bring us to some very dark places indeed. But, in that moment, there was laughter. And while laughter wasn't everything, it was something, and that something was very, very good. As Jetset Ty Rone had said, for the time being at least, this little corner of the universe was all ours, and we were making that shit what we wanted it to be.

At the sound of Neil's indignant howl, Dharmander collapsed into a fit of surprise and delight, slapping the top of the stool next to him with his free palm. "I'm going to end up paying for that," he told us after straightening back up and waving at Neil adoringly, "but it's worth it. Happy birthday!"

Author's Note

Folks who read this story often remark what a good memory I must have to remember all the details of my adventures in Berlin and beyond.

Yes and no. And, also, *maybe.*

Yes, I do have a pretty good memory, especially when it comes to recalling the details of people's personal stories. I'm a good listener and, frankly, tend to enjoy hearing about others' lives more than I like recounting my own. (No, the irony of having written a memoir is not lost on me.) Given this, it's not too surprising that I ended up becoming a cultural anthropologist, a profession that requires one to enter into a state of deep attention, to be alert to research participants' verbal and nonverbal cues, repeated phrases, subtle hints regarding their basic existential assumptions, and so on. This, I'll argue, is even more true when it comes to humanistic anthropology, in which an emphasis is placed on establishing empathetic connections with one's participants and their lived experiences. So, yes...my natural and professional tendency toward entrancement when it comes to OPS (Other People's Stories) most definitely helped me recreate what occurred during the time I spent lurking around Berlin's stand-up comedy scene.

That said, my memory is far from perfect. Fortunately, I have technology on my side. My audio recorder has been my most trusted research companion over the course of my professional career (first cassette, then digital). The majority of quoted conversations in this book were digitally recorded, transcribed, then edited for clarity and pacing. Likewise, the excerpted comedy sets that appear throughout the book are transcriptions of video recordings that Dharmander and Neil generously shared with me after each of the shows I attended. These audio and video recordings allowed me to not only quote conversations and comedy sets word for word, but also to capture essential nonverbal clues (vocal inflections, emotional cues, comedian–audience interactions, body language, and the like) that add to the overall texture of the narrative. After transcribing and editing the recordings, each of the comedians featured had the opportunity to read and make adjustments (mostly minor) to their portion of the text. I thank them all for their participation in this process.

One exception to the above is the character Marianne. "Marianne" is a semi-composite character, created 90 percent out of a real, singular human being, with the remaining 10 percent modeled after two other women I met on the Berlin comedy scene who, like the real Marianne, had some very strong contradictory opinions about my assessment of Cosmic Comedy as "The Friendliest Place in the Universe." For various reasons, these two did not want to be included in the narrative. Their perspective was too important to ignore, so I attributed small sections of these conversations to ones I had with the real Marianne. Since all three women's experiences were so much alike, this choice did not alter the reality of what occurred in any significant way. Also worth noting: Because I was not running my audio recorder when the real Marianne and I hung out together, I recreated our conversations out of memories of what was said, trying to get as close to word for word as possible. Even more important than this, however, was my goal of accurately portraying the *emotional* tone of our encounters. In this, I believe I was successful. Once it was complete, the real Marianne read the manuscript and gave feedback regarding her own memory of things.

There are also areas in which I'm not really sure how good my memory is or isn't. This is particularly the case when it came to describing things that occurred in the distant past. Throughout *The Friendliest Place in the Universe*, I call forth memories of various moments across my life. These are intended to provide context for why the goings on at Cosmic Comedy (and in Berlin in general) ignited my passions in the way that they did. How accurately have I described those moments? Hopefully *very* accurately, but I'm also realistic that memory is an incomplete thing. It floats to the surface of consciousness in fragments, after which the mind, in its desire for narrative completeness, fills in the blanks, assembling a fully formed picture. For example, in Chapter 7, when I recount how my sixth grade classroom smelled like "old milk and puberty," I can say with full certainty that, yes, it *did* smell that way. Trust me, that smell is burned into my brain. Did I consciously notice it on the day of Miss Little's concentric circle exercise? Maybe, maybe not. But it was there, underneath. In other cases in which the details of a past event are hazy, I made well-reasoned guesses. An example of this is in Chapter 1, when I describe my father's shirt as "a 1970's explosion of pink paisley." While I have no clue what color shirt my father was actually wearing on the day that he and I had that talk regarding the nonexistence of God and angels, a photo of him from around that time shows that he did, in fact, own such a shirt. So into the story it went.

Finally, my initial research into the liberation of "collective joy" in January 2018 prompted me to return to Berlin several times over the course of a three-year timespan. Each visit added some new insight that became part of my understanding of the phenomenon. For ease of readability, I have compressed these multiple trips—and their most pertinent insights—into the three-week period recounted within the book.

So, there you have it. In case you were wondering.

About the Author

Hillary S. Webb, PhD, is a cultural anthropologist, author, and mixed-media storyteller. After receiving her undergraduate degree in journalism from New York University, Webb went on to earn an MA in consciousness studies from Goddard College and a PhD in psychology from Saybrook University. Currently a faculty member at Goddard College, she is also the former Managing Editor of *Anthropology of Consciousness*, the peer-reviewed journal of the Society for the Anthropology of Consciousness. She is the author of *Yanantin and Masintin in the Andean World*, *Traveling Between the Worlds*, and *Exploring Shamanism*. When not lurking around the stand-up comedy clubs of Europe, Webb lives in Maine with her husband, photographer Carl Austin Hyatt.

CPSIA information can be obtained
at www.ICGtesting.com
Printed in the USA
LVHW081956250922
729242LV00001B/111

9 781955 737142